WHITEWATER COOKS

the food we love

WHITEWATER COOKS

the food we love

Shelley Adams & Conner Adams

It's no surprise that a son growing up in the kitchen alongside Shelley Adams would develop a similar passion for cooking! In this collection of all-new recipes, Shelley has collaborated with her son, Conner, to create recipes that have Shelley's Kootenay mountain-style tradition meeting Conner's healthy Californian cuisine. Think Wild Mushroom Tarte and Sweet Potato Thai Green Curry with Pappadum-Crusted Halibut or Baklava Cheesecake and Best Key Lime Pie. Together they have created another amazing new Whitewater cookbook with fabulous recipes for everyday living, special occasions and more — it's the food we love!

NANCY WISE, Sandhill Book Marketing Ltd.

Published by **Alicon Holdings Ltd.** Nelson BC

ISBN 978-0-9811424-5-6

All photographs except as noted below copyright © 2024 David R. Gluns. All rights reserved. Pages 155, & 167 top left, by Thomas Nowa. Dave Gluns on page 14 by Gill Stead.

Just as we completed this project, our sweet cat Thomas left us. We honour his beautiful life.

Authors: **Shelley Adams** and **Conner Adams** • whitewatercooks.com
Photography: **David R. Gluns** • gluns.ca
Design and layout: **Gillian Stead**
Edited by: **Marlene Cornelis** • Veranda Editorial

 We eat all the food photographed in our books!

Distributed by **Sandhill Book Marketing,**
sandhillbooks.com • info@sandhillbooks.com

Distributed by **Independent Publishers Group (IPG)** • orders@ipgbook.com
Check out **whitewatercooks.com** to see where you can purchase the series.

Printed and bound in Canada by **Friesens Book Division**

CONTENTS

◆

◆

INTRODUCTION

I remember being just tall enough to see over the counter at my mom's café to order fries. To the left, people could find baked goods like homemade cinnamon buns and granola bars by "Baker Johnny." To the right, you could get a Fancy-Pants Burger or a Black Bean Veggie Burger — real locals would add goat cheese and bacon to this vegan option. Further to the right, you could choose between the daily special, the Ymir Curry Bowl with homemade pappadums, or local favourite mainstays like the now-famous Glory Bowl, Chicken Souvlaki, Runaway Train Wrap, and one of three paninis at a time when nobody in Canada had ever heard the word *panini*.

That food like this was being served at Whitewater, at a time when you couldn't expect more than a dry burger or a slimy hotdog at most ski hills, didn't surprise me, not just because I was young, but also because exposure to good food at home was the norm and expectation.

It wasn't uncommon for us to have artichokes as an after-school snack, and Sundays meant roast chicken with the best, most lemony gravy you could imagine. Every other night of the week brought something new and amazing. Cedar-planked sablefish was a mainstay, as were pan-seared chicken thighs roasted with different, perfectly balanced combinations of sides. Broccoli was often present but always dressed up differently… tossed with toasted sesame oil, crusted with Parmesan, or roasted with pesto.

Then there were the salads. Salads are served after dinner in our family and they were consistently the star of the meal. Each featured the crispiest greens and the perfect combination of nuts, cheese, and dressing. My friends all learned to save room for salad when having dinner at our house.

My mom will be the first to tell you that she's "not crazy about sweets," yet somehow we always found ourselves snacking on a perfect salty cookie or lavender loaf while the tea steeped.

Once it came time for me to leave home and fend for myself, I was worried that these dinners had come to an end. I then had the amazing revelation that I had been given the keys to dine this well on my own — the Whitewater Cooks series. This set of cookbooks has brought me so much joy and good food like it has for any other fan of the series. We hope you'll also love *The Food We Love.* — C.A.

ACKNOWLEDGEMENTS

◆

It's a mother's dream come true to have had an experience with her son that will last a lifetime. Writing and creating this new cookbook together with my son, Conner, was a year that we will always remember, immortalized in the pages and photos of this book. Conner and I share a true love of food and cooking, and collaborating on our recipes to create *The Food We Love* turned our passion into total joy for us. Starting in October 2023, we tested and created recipes in Hawaii, California and British Columbia. We finished in July 2024 with the photo shoots at our home here in the Kootenays where our culinary adventure began! Thank you so much to my talented and amazing son, Conner.

Conner and I would like to express our heartfelt gratitude to our family members Ali, Sarah and Mike for their support, help and love. Ali, as usual, remained constant with her support and advice on any issues that called for her calmness and wisdom. Sarah developed such a smoothly run shooting schedule that we were able to cook and shoot the photos for 68 recipes in three weeks — thanks Sar! Immense thanks and love go to Mike Adams. Conner and I so appreciate all you do, from your thorough recipe testing, endless grocery shopping and proofreading, to of course, the publishing of this book.

Heartfelt thanks to all the friends and family who shared their delicious recipes with Conner and me for this book: Marianne Abraham, Ali Adams, Con Diamond, Nick Diamond, Nathan Faucett, Barb Gosney, Colin Greenlaw, Claire Hitchman, Sarah Johnson, Petra Lehmann, Ryan Martin, Emmy McKnight, Mya Mitchell, Patti Mitchell, Gail Morrison, Melissa Owen, Margie Rosling, Jennifer Schell Lirag, Lisa Shippy, Julia Sydneysmith, Shawn Trainor and Sheri Weichel.

We don't know what we would have done without the amazing, talented and hilarious Emmy McKnight! Emmy wore many hats and excelled at each: recipe tester, food stylist, baker extraordinaire and chef from start to finish. You rule, Emmy — we are forever grateful for your hard work on and dedication to this new book.

To our friend and photographer, David Gluns, thank you with so much love and gratitude. We've worked side by side with David for seven books now and he's photographed over 650 recipes! We so appreciate his passion and dedication to the Whitewater Cooks series. This book's shooting team of David, Conner, Sarah, Emmy and me was the best one yet!

To the designer of *The Food We Love*, Gill Stead, you are a true professional and a joy to work with. Your design work is truly a thing of beauty. Thanks for coming all the way to Nelson to be part of the photo shoot process. Eating dinner together at our favourite restaurant, the Main Street Diner, was really the best way to get to see why we love living here!

To Marlene Cornelis, thank you for your impeccable editing skills and your many insightful questions that helped us hone our recipes for the readers' benefit.

To Nancy Wise, thank you so much for all your dedication to the marketing and selling of the Whitewater Cooks series. We can't thank you enough for all you do for us.

Thank you so much to Yuki Conne for the beautiful bowls you made for the clam recipe in this book!

And to the Whitewater Cooks fans, we thank you all. You keep us going! — S.A.

STARTERS

◆

Coconut Curry Clams 18

Ricotta and Pine Nut Meatballs with Marinara Sauce 20

Pimento Cheese
with Nathan's Jalapeno Southern Cornbread 22

Mediterranean Green Olive Grilled Prawns 24

Prosciutto Rolls with Figs and Arugula 26

Marinated Manchego Cheese Antipasto 28

Buffalo Cauliflower Bites
and Good Ol' Chicken Wings with Ranch Dip 30

Mexican Street Corn
with Homemade Tortilla Chips 32

Jennifer's Wild Mushroom Tarte 34

Tuna Crudo with Citrus and Capers 36

Carne Asada Tostadas 38

◆

Coconut Curry
CLAMS

We love fresh clams! Growing up on the west coast of British Columbia, eating clams was a common occurrence for all of us. Here's a twist on the usual straight-up steamed clams with tons of garlic butter that we always ate as a family!   •   SERVES 4

INGREDIENTS

36 butter, littleneck, or similar clams
2 tbsp sea salt, plus more as needed, divided
1 tbsp olive oil
2 medium shallots, diced
4 cloves garlic, minced
1 1-inch knob ginger, peeled and minced
1 bunch cilantro, stems and leaves
  finely chopped, leaves divided
1 tbsp red or yellow Thai curry paste
1 13-oz can coconut milk
½ cup chicken or vegetable stock
2 limes, freshly squeezed
sea salt and freshly ground pepper
1 baguette of your choice

METHOD

Scrub clams under cold water to remove any grit.

Combine the 2 tbsp sea salt with 4 cups of cold water and submerge clams. If all the clams aren't submerged, add additional salted water until they are, maintaining the same ratio of salt to water.

Soak the clams for at least 20 minutes or up to 2 hours to allow them to expel any sand held within the shells.

Remove the clams from the water and quickly rinse under cold water to remove any discarded sand that may be on the outside of the shells.

Pour olive oil into a large pot over medium-high heat.

Sauté the shallots, garlic and ginger for 10 minutes, or until they turn slightly golden, stirring frequently.

Stir in the cilantro stems.

Add curry paste and stir to coat the shallots. Cook for 2 minutes.

Pour in coconut milk and stock and bring to a simmer for a few minutes.

Add all the clams to the pot and cook until they've opened, approximately 10 minutes, discarding any that stay closed.

Stir in the cilantro leaves.

Season with lime juice, and salt and pepper to taste.

These clams are delicious served with a crusty baguette, basmati rice or some linguine, to make them more of a meal.

RICOTTA and PINE NUT MEATBALLS
with Marinara Sauce

We love a plate of saucy meatballs as a starter. Often, people need more than just cheese or vegetables before the actual dinner begins! The ricotta and crunchy pine nuts in this recipe make it delicious. Thanks to Margie, the queen of cooking and entertaining at the drop of a hat, for these beauties! • SERVES 4–6 (MAKES 2 DOZEN MEATBALLS)

INGREDIENTS

Meatballs

¾ cup whole milk ricotta
½ cup panko bread crumbs
1 tbsp olive oil
½ medium yellow or sweet onion, Šnely diced
1 head garlic (about 8 cloves), peeled and minced
¾ lb lean ground beef
¾ lb medium ground pork or ground veal
2 eggs
¾ cup Parmesan, grated
½ cup pine nuts, toasted and Šnely chopped
⅓ cup basil, finely chopped, plus more for garnish
¼ cup Italian parsley, finely chopped,
   plus more for garnish
1½ tbsp Italian seasoning
1 tsp crushed red pepper flakes
1½ tsp kosher salt
1 tsp freshly ground pepper

Marinara Sauce

¼ cup olive oil, plus more for drizzling
½ medium yellow onion, Šnely chopped
4 large cloves garlic, minced
½ tsp kosher salt
¼ tsp freshly ground pepper
¼ tsp crushed red pepper flakes
2 tbsp tomato paste
4–6 anchovy fillets (optional)
¼ cup dry white wine
1 28-oz can top quality tomato sauce
   or whole tomatoes (San Marzano are great)
½ cup fresh basil, coarsely chopped
Parmesan, grated, for garnish

METHOD

Meatballs

Preheat oven to 400°F.

Mix panko and ricotta in a bowl and combine well. Set aside for 15 minutes.

Pour olive oil into a frying pan over medium heat, add onion and cook for about 5 minutes, stirring frequently, or until softened.

Stir in garlic and cook for another 2 minutes. Remove from heat and set aside.

Place beef and pork in a large mixing bowl and add the sautéed onions, ricotta mixture, eggs, Parmesan, pine nuts, herbs, Italian seasoning, red pepper flakes, salt and pepper.

Mix with your hands (*take care not to overmix*).

Form meatballs with an ice cream scoop. Transfer, evenly spaced, to a parchment-lined baking sheet. Bake for 10 minutes, then broil for 5–7 minutes until golden brown.

Marinara Sauce

Pour oil into a heavy-bottomed large pot and heat on medium-high until smoking.

Add onion to the hot oil — it should really sizzle! Sauté until it begins to brown, then reduce heat to medium low. Add garlic, salt, pepper and pepper flakes. Cook for 2 minutes.

Add tomato paste and anchovies, if using.

Stir until everything's well coated with paste.

Cook for an additional 2–3 minutes before adding wine to deglaze.

Cook for 2–3 more minutes to cook off the alcohol and reduce wine by half.

Add tomato sauce or whole tomatoes and their juices (crushing by hand as you add them) and basil.

Bring to a simmer, then reduce heat to low and simmer for 35–40 minutes.

Remove from heat and adjust the salt, pepper, oil and pepper flakes to taste.

Transfer the sauce to a blender or food processor and blend until smooth.

TO SERVE

Spoon warm marinara sauce onto a serving dish, drizzle with a bit of oil and sprinkle on some grated Parmesan.

Top with meatballs and garnish with basil, parsley, Parmesan, and salt and pepper to taste.

Everyone needs a good mother sauce like marinara in their repertoire. Double or quadruple this versatile recipe and freeze to use in so many great dinners, like lasagna, a quick prawn pasta, Bolognese sauce, eggplant Parmesan or pizza sauce!

PIMENTO CHEESE
with Nathan's Jalapeno Southern Cornbread

Conner's wife, Sarah, is from South Carolina and has taught us all that pimento cheese is found on everyone's table in the South. She shared this authentic recipe with us. Her brother-in-law Nathan, the sweetest Southern boy ever, shared his mom's cornbread recipe. Together they are a winner and a true Southern way to begin a meal. • SERVES 8

INGREDIENTS

Cornbread

2¾ cups cornmeal
3 tbsp baking powder
1½ tsp salt
3 tbsp sugar
3 eggs, room temperature
½ teaspoon baking soda
½ cup neutral oil, melted butter or shortening
½ large onion, Šnely diced
1½ cups cheddar, shredded
2 jalapeno peppers, finely chopped
(remove seeds for less spiciness)
1 cup frozen corn, cooked and drained
1 red pepper, finely diced
½–1 cup milk

Pimento Cheese

4 oz cream cheese, room temperature
½ cup mayonnaise
½ tsp hot sauce
½ tsp kosher salt
¼ tsp sugar
¼ tsp smoked paprika
⅛ tsp cayenne pepper
⅛ tsp white pepper
1 4-oz jar diced pimento peppers and brine
1 lb quality sharp cheddar, coarsely shredded
1 fresh serrano pepper, diced (optional)

METHOD

Cornbread

Preheat oven to 400°F.

Mix all ingredients except milk in a large bowl.

Stir in just enough milk for the mixture to hold together well.

Spread the batter in a greased 9 × 13-inch pan and bake for 30–35 minutes, or until golden brown.

Let rest for an hour for best results (the cornbread will hold together better).

Pimento Cheese

Combine cream cheese and mayonnaise in a mixing bowl.

Add hot sauce, salt, sugar, spices, pimento peppers and brine, and cheddar. Stir well.

Fold in serrano pepper, if using.

Place in a serving dish.

TO SERVE

Spread the pimento cheese on the cornbread.

Nathan's mom Anne first found the cornbread recipe on the back of a Martha White Yellow Cornmeal bag and made a few changes over the years. She used to serve it with pinto or butter beans and turnip greens. It goes great with BBQ or chili, and is perfect for anyone looking to add a little spice to their cornbread.

Mediterranean Green Olive
GRILLED PRAWNS

This green olive dressing has been a favourite salad dressing of ours for years,
and thank goodness Conner had the great idea of spooning it over some grilled prawns! • SERVES 4-6

INGREDIENTS

Green Olive Dressing

1 cup Castelvetrano green olives,
   pitted and roughly chopped
1 garlic clove, minced
1 green onion,
   thinly sliced diagonally
1 lemon, zest and juice of
1 shallot, finely diced
2 cups loosely packed herb leaves
   (preferably a mix of Italian parsley
   and mint), finely chopped
3 tbsp white or red wine vinegar
¾ cup extra-virgin olive oil
½ tsp sea salt or to taste
½ tsp freshly ground pepper
   or to taste

Prawns

12–16 large whole prawns
2 tbsp olive oil
¼ tsp sea salt or to taste
¼ tsp freshly ground pepper
   or to taste

METHOD

Green Olive Dressing

Place the olives, garlic, green onion, lemon zest and juice, shallot,
chopped herbs and vinegar in a medium-sized mixing bowl.
Stir in olive oil.
Season the herby olive mixture with salt and pepper to taste.

Prawns

Preheat barbecue or grill to 400°F.
Toss prawns in a large bowl with oil, salt and pepper.
Grill for about 3 minutes per side, or until pink, or sauté in a frying pan
over medium-high heat for about 3 minutes per side, or until cooked.

TO SERVE

Place the prawns on serving plates
or a platter and spoon the
Green Olive Dressing over top.

You'll probably have leftover dressing to enjoy on your salad greens the next day.

PROSCIUTTO ROLLS
with Figs and Arugula

There are so many gluten-free friends and family members these days that this simple treat will be popular
in your appetizer repertoire. Prosciutto slices are usually paper thin, but for this recipe be sure they're not too thin
or they'll tear when you spread the cheese on them. Fresh figs would be amazing here if you can find them.
Bring out the chilled Pinot Grigio! • MAKES 12 BITES

INGREDIENTS

¼ cup extra-virgin olive oil
1 lemon, zest of
2 tbsp freshly squeezed lemon juice
12 slices prosciutto
8 oz goat cheese, room temperature
18 dried black mission figs, quartered
½ tsp freshly ground pepper
4 cups arugula, stems trimmed
balsamic crema to drizzle

METHOD

Whisk oil, lemon juice and zest in a
medium-sized bowl to blend.
Lay prosciutto slices on the work surface,
spacing slices 2 inches apart.
Spread goat cheese evenly over prosciutto.
Arrange figs over cheese, dividing and spacing evenly.
Drizzle olive oil and lemon mixture over the figs
and cheese and sprinkle with pepper.
Arrange 6 arugula leaves on each prosciutto slice,
alternating stems and tops and allowing tops
to extend 1 inch over the meat's long sides .
Roll up tightly like a jelly roll, starting at one end
of each slice.
Transfer to a serving platter.
Drizzle each roll with some balsamic crema.

These can be made 2 hours ahead of time.
Cover with damp paper towels and then plastic wrap and
chill. Reserve the balsamic drizzle until just before serving.

If there are a few vegetarians in the crowd, you could also use thinly sliced zucchini instead of the prosciutto.

Marinated
MANCHEGO CHEESE ANTIPASTO

This cheery and colourful dip reminds us of being in Spain. With a cold glass of prosecco in hand and a spoonful of this dip on your favourite crackers, you're set! • SERVES 4–6

INGREDIENTS

4 tbsp extra-virgin olive oil
1 tbsp Calabrian chili peppers
  or pepperoncini peppers, chopped
4 garlic cloves, minced
¾ cup Manchego, crumbled (about ¼ lb)
2 tbsp jarred roasted red peppers, chopped
2 tbsp jarred sun-dried tomatoes, chopped
1 tbsp Italian parsley, chopped
1 tbsp red wine vinegar
sea salt and freshly ground pepper

METHOD

Mix oil, chili peppers and garlic in a small pot.
Simmer over low heat for 15–20 minutes to infuse the oil. There should be small bubbles, but the oil should never boil.
Place Manchego in a small bowl and pour the infused oil over it.
Add red peppers, tomatoes, parsley and vinegar to the bowl and mix.
Season with salt and pepper to taste.

Put the marinated Manchego in your favourite jar or sealed container and take on a picnic, to the ski hill, or out on the boat!

Buffalo CAULIFLOWER BITES and Good Ol' CHICKEN WINGS with Ranch Dip

These cauliflower bites have the same great flavours and crispiness as the traditional chicken wings, with a nice cool dip to complement their hotness. This is a great starter for any occasion, any time of the year. Having both choices on your serving platter is a win-win situation. Hurray for cauliflower! Hurray for wings! • SERVES 6

INGREDIENTS

Cauliflower and Chicken Wings

1 cup olive oil
1 cup hot sauce,
    such as Franks RedHot or sriracha
4 tsp smoked paprika
2 tsp freshly ground pepper
2 tsp garlic powder
pinch sea salt
1 large head cauliflower, broken into florets
    (about 6 cups)
18 chicken wings, split, wing tips discarded
1½ cups panko bread crumbs
¾ cup Parmesan, grated

Jalapeno Ranch Dip

1 large lime, freshly squeezed
¼ tsp sea salt
¼ tsp freshly ground pepper
1 cup plain yogurt (plant based if desired)
2 large garlic cloves, finely minced
1 tbsp dried dill
1 jalapeno, seeded and coarsely chopped
    (keep the seeds if you want more spice)
2 tbsp fresh cilantro, chopped
½ tsp smoked paprika, for garnish

METHOD

Cauliflower and Chicken Wings

Preheat oven to 425°F.
Combine oil, hot sauce, paprika, pepper, garlic powder and salt in a large bowl and transfer half to a second bowl.
Place cauliflower in one bowl and chicken wings in the other. Toss each to coat well.
Combine bread crumbs and Parmesan in another bowl.
Dredge the cauliflower and then the chicken wings in the bread crumb mixture, pressing to make the crumbs stick. Place on separate parchment-lined baking sheets.
Roast for 40–45 minutes, or until the cauliflower is tender and golden brown and the chicken wings are golden brown and cooked through.

Jalapeno Ranch Dip

Purée all ingredients except paprika in a food processor until smooth. Adjust salt and pepper to taste, transfer to a serving bowl, and garnish with paprika or more dill.

TO SERVE

Serve the cauliflower bites and wings with the refreshing and zesty dip, and satisfy everyone around the kitchen island!

Instead of discarding the chicken wing tips, you could save them to use in your next batch of stock.

MEXICAN STREET CORN
with Homemade Tortilla Chips

Creamy, tangy, spicy, crisp, juicy and sweet! Mexican street corn is another name for elotes, grilled whole cobs of corn topped with mayonnaise, hot sauce or chili powder, lime and cotija cheese. These beauties can be found all over the streets of Mexico. This is a version of the authentic elotes turned into a fab dip for tortilla chips. It's best made with whole cobs of corn grilled on the barbecue, but you can also use cooked corn niblets if you'd rather not turn on the grill. • SERVES 4

INGREDIENTS

Mexican Street Corn

4 ears corn, or 4 cups cooked
  and cooled corn niblets
extra-virgin olive oil, for brushing
2 tbsp mayonnaise
1 garlic clove, minced
1 lime, zest and juice of
½ cup green onions, thinly sliced
½ cup cotija, crumbled
¼ cup cilantro, chopped
½ tsp smoked paprika or chili powder
1 jalapeno, finely diced
½ tsp sea salt or to taste

Homemade Tortilla Chips

1 package thin 10-inch white flour
  or whole wheat tortillas
2 cups neutral oil, such as canola or avocado
sea salt or kosher salt

METHOD

Mexican Street Corn

Preheat the barbecue to medium-high heat.

Brush corn with oil and grill for 2 minutes per side, or until grill marks appear. Remove from the barbecue and set aside.

Combine mayonnaise, garlic, and lime zest and juice in a large bowl.

Slice the kernels off the cobs and add to the bowl. Stir to coat, then mix in green onions, cotija, cilantro, paprika, jalapeno and salt. Taste and add more salt if desired.

Serve right away, or chill until needed.

Homemade Tortilla Chips

Line a baking sheet with a couple sheets of paper towel and place close to your stovetop. Have a pair of tongs and salt handy.

Cut each tortilla into 16 wedges.

Heat oil in a heavy-bottomed pot until hot but not smoking (test it with a piece of tortilla — it should float to the top and start to turn golden quite quickly.)

Drop a handful of wedges into the hot oil carefully and use your tongs to move them around. When nicely browned, remove them with the tongs and place on the paper-towel-lined pan.

Sprinkle the hot chips with salt to taste.

Repeat until all the chips are done.

We love this Mexican street corn as a salad too!

Jennifer's
WILD MUSHROOM TARTE

Thanks to Jennifer Schell Lirag, author of four fabulous cookbooks and an amazing force of nature in every way, for this recipe.
We added some sherry and goat cheese and we're going wild for it! • SERVES 4–6

INGREDIENTS

1 tbsp butter
½ medium sweet onion,
   halved lengthwise and thinly sliced
1 clove garlic, minced
1 tbsp olive oil
2½ cups wild mushrooms, roughly chopped
2 tbsp sherry (optional)
2 tsp fresh thyme, chopped
sea salt and freshly ground black pepper
1 sheet frozen puff pastry,
   thawed in the fridge overnight
1½ cups Gruyère, grated
4 oz goat cheese, crumbled
smoked Maldon salt (optional)
thyme leaves, for garnish

METHOD

Preheat oven to 375°F.

Heat a large frying pan over medium-low heat and add butter.

Add onions and garlic and sauté for 2–3 minutes, or until softened.

Remove from heat and transfer the mixture to a bowl.

Wipe the pan and return to the burner. Increase heat to medium-high. Pour in olive oil and then add mushrooms in a single layer. Do not stir for 1–2 minutes to allow mushrooms to sear and brown — this is important!

Stir and cook for 2–3 more minutes, or until softened and golden.

Add sherry, if using, and cook for a few more minutes until the liquid has absorbed into the mushrooms.

Remove from heat and add to the bowl with the onions and garlic and set aside to cool. Stir in the chopped thyme and season with salt and pepper to taste.

Unroll puff pastry onto a parchment-lined baking sheet. Using a sharp paring knife, lightly score a border around the entire edge (don't cut all the way through the dough). Using a fork, prick all over the surface within the border and crimp the edges.

Distribute Gruyère evenly within the pastry's border and sprinkle goat cheese on top. Top with the cooled mushroom and onion mixture.

Bake for 25–30 minutes, or until golden brown.

Sprinkle with smoked salt and thyme leaves.

Cool, cut into pieces and serve!

Always have a package of puff pastry in your freezer.
You can whip up so many good things that will impress your friends at wine o'clock!

TUNA CRUDO
with Citrus and Capers

We love fresh raw fish with the simplest of ingredients.
The citrus and capers work well together to create this easy-peasy version of tuna crudo. • SERVES 4

INGREDIENTS

1 lb ahi tuna, sushi grade
1 lemon, juice of
1 orange, juice of
2 tbsp caper brine
2 tbsp capers
1 Persian cucumber, thinly sliced
1 tsp sesame seeds, toasted
1 tbsp extra-virgin olive oil

METHOD

Slice tuna thinly and place on a long rectangular platter.

Stir together lemon and orange juices, caper brine and capers in a small bowl.

Pour over tuna when ready to serve and top with sliced cucumbers and sesame seeds.

Drizzle with olive oil.

Have a few rice crackers on hand if you'd like a platform for your slices of tuna.
Otherwise, bring out some chopsticks and you're good to go!

Carne Asada
TOSTADAS

We love all the amazing Mexican food of Los Angeles! Everything is so authentic and you can find so many dishes that we don't see very often up here in Canada. Carne asada is a perfect backyard barbecue dish. Here, you slice it up very thinly and serve it individually on perfectly crunchy tostadas. • MAKES 8-12 TOSTADAS

INGREDIENTS

1 flank steak (1½-2 lbs)
8-12 tostadas, store-bought
   or homemade
2 limes, juice of

Marinade

3 limes, juice of
1 orange, juice of
2 tsp Mexican or regular oregano
sea salt
⅓ cup olive oil
4 garlic cloves, minced
3 tsp chipotle pepper
   in adobo sauce, finely chopped

Sour Cream

1 cup sour cream
3 tsp chipotle pepper
   in adobo sauce, finely chopped
sea salt

Garnish

1 white onion, finely chopped
1 bunch cilantro, finely chopped
   (about ½ cup)
1 lime

METHOD

Mix all marinade ingredients, including salt to taste, then submerge flank steak in the marinade and refrigerate for 1-2 hours.

Mix sour cream ingredients, including salt to taste, in a small bowl and set aside.

Mix garnish ingredients in a small bowl and set aside.

Preheat the barbecue to high heat and lightly oil the grill.

Remove flank steak from marinade and grill on each side for 3-4 minutes for rare to medium rare.

Remove from heat and let rest for 10 minutes.

Slice the beef as thinly as you can against the grain.

TO SERVE

Spread some sour cream to cover most of one side of a tostada, top with a few strips of thinly sliced beef, and garnish with the onion cilantro mixture.

Repeat with the remaining tostadas.

Squeeze some fresh lime on top of each tostada.

Some small choices here make a huge difference! Make sure you use white onions, and try your best to cook the flank steak rare to medium rare. This plus the Mexican Street Corn (page 32) is a perfect combination.

SOUPS & SIDES

◆

◆

PETRA'S ROASTED CAULIFLOWER
with Crispy Pancetta and Olive Dressing

Our treasured friend Petra shared this recipe with us a few years ago and it seriously is one of our favourite dishes in the world. It's so delicious paired with sablefish or salmon, but also fabulous with just a bowl of basmati rice. Thank you Petra, we miss you every single day. • SERVES 4

INGREDIENTS

1 large head cauliflower, trimmed and
   cut into bite-sized florets (about 8 cups)
½ cup extra-virgin olive oil, divided
½ tsp Maldon salt, plus more as needed
⅓ cup green or kalamata olives,
   crushed, pitted and chopped
1 large garlic clove, minced or finely grated
1 lemon, juice of, plus more as needed
¼ tsp crushed red pepper flakes,
   plus more as needed
¼ cup parsley, chopped
4 ounces pancetta or bacon,
   cut into ⅛-inch cubes
¾ tsp cumin seeds
½ cup Parmesan, grated

METHOD

Preheat oven to 425°F.

Place cauliflower on a parchment-lined baking sheet and toss with ¼ cup olive oil and ½ tsp salt until well coated.

Roast for 10 minutes. Toss and return to oven for 10 minutes.

Mix together the olives, garlic, lemon juice, pepper flakes, parsley and a large pinch of salt in a small bowl. Pour in the remaining ¼ cup olive oil, whisk well and set aside.

Remove cauliflower from the oven, sprinkle with pancetta and cumin seeds, and gently mix to combine.

Sprinkle Parmesan on top and roast for another 15–20 minutes, or until cauliflower is tender and cheese is golden brown and crispy.

Spoon the olive dressing all over the cauliflower while still hot and toss to combine.

Taste and add more salt, red pepper flakes or lemon juice if needed.

To make this an equally delicious vegetarian side dish simply omit the pancetta.

PEPPERY SWEET POTATOES
with Creamy Dill Yogurt

This dish is the perfect side to serve with just about anything.
The smoky pepperiness of the sweet potatoes is perfectly balanced by the creamy dill yogurt.   •   SERVES 4

INGREDIENTS

2 medium to large sweet potatoes
3 tbsp extra-virgin olive oil
1 tbsp gochugaru chili flakes
    or ½ tbsp crushed red pepper flakes
½ tbsp smoked paprika
1 tbsp honey
2 limes, juice of, divided
sea salt and freshly ground pepper
¾ cup full-fat plain yogurt
1 large clove garlic, minced
1 tbsp dried dill
3 green onions, thinly sliced on the bias

METHOD

Preheat oven to 400°F.

Wash sweet potatoes and slice each lengthwise into 8 wedges.

Stir together oil, chili flakes, paprika, honey and half the lime juice in a large mixing bowl.

Toss the sweet potato wedges in the mixture to coat and place on a parchment-lined baking sheet.

Season with salt and pepper, then drizzle any leftover marinade over the sweet potatoes.

Roast for 30 minutes, or until tender.

Mix yogurt, garlic, dill and the remaining lime juice, and season with salt and pepper to taste.

Serve sweet potatoes with plenty of yogurt spooned on top and garnish with the sliced green onions.

Of course, you could make these with good ol' russet potatoes too!

Mushroom & Kale
YUZU FARRO

Our friend Petra loved this side dish and ate it hot or cold. She often thanked Conner for creating it!
This is for you, dear Petie.   •   SERVES 4

INGREDIENTS

4 tbsp extra-virgin olive oil
1 large yellow onion, finely diced
2 cloves garlic, finely grated using a microplane
2 small carrots, washed and finely grated
sea salt and freshly ground pepper
2 tbsp gochugaru chili flakes,
   or 1 tsp crushed red chili flakes
1 tbsp za'atar
2 large portobello mushrooms, thinly sliced
2 cups shiitake mushrooms, thinly sliced
1 cup farro
1 cup vegetable stock
2 tbsp apple cider vinegar
2 tbsp yuzu kosho paste or juice
1 large bunch kale, torn into bite sized pieces
   (about 2 cups)

METHOD

Heat olive oil in a large pot over medium-high heat.
Add onion, garlic and carrots and season with
salt and pepper to taste.
Sauté 4–5 minutes until translucent, then mix in
gochugaru and za'atar.
Add mushrooms, mix well and sauté for an
additional 2 minutes.
Stir in farro and cook for 3–4 minutes, until farro
is lightly browned in places and smells toasty.
Add vegetable stock, 2 cups water, vinegar and
yuzu kosho paste.
Bring to a boil, reduce heat and simmer for 30–40
minutes, until farro has absorbed all the liquid.
Remove from heat, stir in kale, and let sit for
5–10 minutes before serving.

*A microplane is an excellent tool for zesting citrus fruit
or finely grating foods such as vegetables and cheese.*

Roast chicken would be awesome with this amazing farro! Spice blends and condiments
like gochugaru, za'atar and yuzu kosho can be found in most specialty food stores.

Ali's CANNELLINI BEANS and ROASTED SQUASH

with Crispy Sage Leaves

Ali Adams is a busy lawyer who needs to be able to make a fast but healthy and flavourful little dinner or side dish in a flash. Here's her rustic Tuscan recipe that you'll be glad to have in your back pocket! • SERVES 4

INGREDIENTS

1 butternut squash, skin on, seeded, cut into ½-inch-thick semicircles
4 tbsp olive oil, divided
sea salt and freshly ground pepper, plus some cracked
12 sage leaves
4 cloves garlic, minced
2 14-oz cans cannellini beans, drained and rinsed
1½ cups vegetable or bone broth
sourdough bread, sliced and toasted

METHOD

Preheat oven to 400°F.

Toss squash pieces with 2 tbsp olive oil and season with salt and pepper to taste.

Roast squash on a parchment-lined baking sheet for 35–40 minutes, flipping the pieces halfway through.

Heat the remaining 2 tbsp olive oil in a large pan over medium heat.

Crisp the sage leaves in the olive oil for 2–3 minutes, then remove from the pan and set aside.

Sweat minced garlic in the oil for 1–2 minutes, then stir in beans and vegetable broth.

Season with salt and pepper to taste and simmer for 6–7 minutes, or until thick.

TO SERVE

Top beans with squash and sage leaves, plus freshly cracked pepper and a piece of sourdough bread for each person.

Ali makes this with bone broth for extra protein and collagen.

Sarah's
LEMON RISOTTO

Sarah made us this lemony risotto in Maui one Christmas and we all loved it! Having a batch of homemade preserved lemons in your fridge is always a bonus, but most grocery stores carry them these days. • SERVES 4

INGREDIENTS

2 tsp sea salt
2 tbsp extra-virgin olive oil
1 large shallot, finely chopped
1½ cups arborio or other risotto rice
½ cup white wine
1 preserved lemon, finely diced,
  or 2 lemons, zest and juice of
1 bunch basil, chopped
½ cup Parmesan, grated
coarsely ground pepper

METHOD

Combine 2 tsp salt with 6 cups water in a medium pot and heat until just simmering.

Heat oil in a cast-iron pan over medium-high heat, and sauté shallot 2–3 minutes, or until soft.

Stir in rice to coat with oil.

Sauté 2–3 minutes, then add wine and cook until the alcohol has burned off and wine is mostly evaporated.

Ladle in simmering salted water patiently, ½ cup at a time. Cook over a lively simmer, stirring constantly, waiting until each addition is absorbed into the rice before adding more.

Check for doneness when you've added most of the water, after about 20–30 minutes. The risotto should be soft and creamy, but al dente.

Add a bit more water if you like your risotto creamier.

Turn off the heat and add lemon, basil and Parmesan.

Taste and, if necessary, season with a bit more salt.

Serve with a generous grating of pepper and a drizzle of your favourite olive oil.

A piece of grilled salmon and a simple arugula and shaved fennel salad
would turn this yummy risotto into a perfect meal.

Chard, Leek and Brie
GRATIN

This is a fancier and healthier version of scalloped potatoes.
Conner serves this side dish with barbecued ribs or a roast chicken. • SERVES 8

INGREDIENTS

2 bunches Swiss or rainbow chard
2 large leeks
1 red onion, thinly sliced
2 tbsp olive oil, divided
sea salt and freshly ground pepper
½ tsp balsamic vinegar
2 tbsp fresh thyme leaves
butter or olive oil,
    for greasing the baking dish
3 lb Yukon Gold potatoes, thinly
    sliced (⅛ inch) on a mandoline
1 cup full-fat milk
10 oz brie, cut into ½-inch cubes
3 tbsp cold butter, cut into
    small pieces
2 cups Parmesan, grated
⅓ cup fresh bread crumbs

METHOD

Preheat oven to 375°F.
Remove stems from chard, roughly chop and set aside. Coarsely chop leaves and set aside separately.
Chop any dark green parts off leeks and discard. Cut leeks in half lengthwise, then wash well to remove any dirt.
Slice halved leeks crosswise, then wash again to remove any remaining dirt. Set aside along with sliced onion.
Heat 1 tbsp olive oil in a large frying pan over medium-high heat and sauté the chard leaves for 4–5 minutes, or until soft. Set cooked chard aside and add the remaining 1 tbsp oil to the pan.
Sauté the chard stems, leeks and onion for about 6 minutes, or until softened.
Sprinkle with salt and pepper to taste, then add vinegar and cook for an additional 2–3 minutes, or until vinegar is absorbed.
Mix chard leaves and thyme leaves into the leek and onion mixture.
Remove from heat and set aside.
Grease the bottom and sides of a 9 ×13-inch baking dish with butter or olive oil, or some of both.

Make the first layer of the gratin as follows in the next four steps.
Spread a third of the sliced potatoes evenly along the base of the dish and season generously with salt and pepper to taste.
Pour ⅓ cup milk evenly over the potatoes.
Evenly distribute a quarter of the brie, butter, and Parmesan over potatoes.
Spread a third of the chard, onion and thyme mixture over top.
Make two more gratin layers, reserving a quarter of the cheeses and butter for the top.
Top with remaining butter and cheese, and sprinkle the bread crumbs over the top layer.
Cover the baking dish with foil and bake for 60 minutes.
Remove the foil, increase the heat to 400°F, and bake for an additional 30 minutes, or until the top is golden brown and crispy.
Remove from the oven and let sit for at least 30 minutes.
Cut into individual squares.

You can make this gratin the day before and reheat at 400°F for 30 minutes.

Smashed

WALDORF POTATOES

Mike's Special Potatoes from the Whitewater Cooks *More Beautiful Food* cookbook are so friggin' good that
we decided to include another version in *The Food We Love*. We can't get enough of this technique for these little potatoes.
The blue cheese and candied walnuts make this dish feel like a dessert as much as a side! • SERVES 4–6

INGREDIENTS

Potatoes
20–24 nugget or baby potatoes
4 tbsp extra-virgin olive oil, divided
sea salt

Blue Cheese Cream
1 cup roquefort, crumbled
½ cup sour cream
1 tsp white wine vinegar
sea salt and freshly ground pepper

Candied Walnuts
1 tbsp butter
½ cup walnuts, roughly chopped
    and toasted
sea salt and freshly ground pepper
1 tbsp maple syrup
2 tbsp fresh tarragon or parsley,
    chopped

METHOD

Potatoes
Preheat oven to 400°F.
Place potatoes in a pot of cold water, bring
to a boil and reduce heat to medium-high.
Cook for about 20 minutes, until potatoes
are just done and can be pierced with a fork.
Drain potatoes right away and place on a
parchment-lined baking sheet.
Gently smash and flatten potatoes
with a meat mallet or the back of
a wooden spoon.
Drizzle with 2 tbsp oil and sprinkle
with salt to taste.
Roast for 15 minutes, flip, drizzle with
the remaining 2 tbsp oil and roast for
another 15 minutes.
Remove from the oven.

Blue Cheese Cream
Combine roquefort, sour cream and
vinegar in a medium-sized bowl and
season with salt and pepper to taste.
This can be done with a whisk or a
fork to break down the blue cheese
crumbles and achieve a creamy
consistency.

Candied Walnuts
Melt butter in a small frying pan
over medium heat.
Toss walnuts in butter for
2–3 minutes, then season with
salt and pepper to taste.
Turn off heat, add maple syrup
and stir to coat walnuts. Set aside.

TO SERVE

Spread blue cheese cream on a serving platter.
Arrange potatoes on top.
Sprinkle with candied walnuts and garnish with tarragon.

This is the perfect fancy side for your favourite steak.

CARROT GINGER SOUP
with Buttery Peas

Conner makes this favourite version of carrot ginger soup topped with a big pile of peas. Shelley swears that she didn't make him finish his peas before he left the table as a child — he's just always loved them!   •   SERVES 6–8

INGREDIENTS

2 tbsp extra-virgin olive oil
1 yellow onion, diced
6 cloves garlic, crushed
sea salt and freshly ground pepper
1 3-inch piece ginger,
    peeled and finely grated
1 tbsp ground turmeric
2 lb carrots, peeled and grated,
    6–8 cups loosely packed
3 cups vegetable stock
2 14-oz cans coconut milk
1 tbsp apple cider vinegar
3 cups peas (frozen is fine)
1½ tbsp salted butter

METHOD

Heat oil in a heavy-bottomed pot over medium heat.

Sauté onion and garlic in oil for 2–3 minutes, then season with salt and pepper to taste.

Stir in ginger and turmeric and cook for another 2–3 minutes, or until onion is soft and spices are fragrant.

Add grated carrots and cook for 10 minutes, stirring occasionally.

Add vegetable stock and coconut milk, bring to a simmer, and cook for 25–30 minutes.

Purée in a blender, or blend with an immersion stick until smooth.

Add the puréed soup back to the pot over medium-low heat and bring it back to temperature.

Add vinegar and season with more salt and lots of pepper.

Heat peas in a microwave or pot of boiling water, strain off any excess liquid, add butter and let it melt.

Serve the soup hot with a scoop of the buttery peas on top and plenty of cracked pepper.

This soup is a much more fun way to get your peas and carrots!

HEALING
Chicken Soup

This version of chicken soup involves simmering a whole chicken,
which is the reason why it's really good for both healing and the soul!   •   SERVES 8–10

INGREDIENTS

3 tbsp neutral oil, such as canola or avocado
5 green onions, thinly sliced crosswise
5 garlic cloves, minced
3 tbsp peeled and grated fresh ginger
    (about 1 3-inch piece)
4 tsp ground coriander
1 tbsp ground turmeric
2 tsp sea salt, plus more as needed
freshly ground pepper
1½ cups short-grain brown or arborio rice
12 cups chicken stock
1 whole chicken (3–4 lbs), wings and legs
    removed and set aside
3 bunches baby bok choy (about 1 lb),
    cut into bite-sized pieces
sliced fresh red chili pepper, julienned
    fresh ginger, and chopped cilantro
    for garnish (optional)

METHOD

Pour oil into a large heavy-bottomed pot over medium-low heat.
Add sliced green onion, garlic, ginger, coriander and turmeric.
Season with salt and pepper to taste and stir for about 5 minutes,
or until slightly softened.
Add rice and stir until coated. Add chicken stock and 2 tsp salt
and bring to a boil over high heat.
Reduce heat to medium-low when the stock comes to a boil.
Carefully add whole chicken, then wings and legs. Add water
if needed to fully submerge chicken meat.
Cover the pot with a lid, leaving it cracked open about an inch,
and simmer over medium-low heat 20–25 minutes, or until
chicken is cooked through. Reduce the heat to low if necessary
to maintain a low simmer so the chicken stays tender.
Transfer chicken to a large bowl and let cool.
Continue to cook the soup uncovered over medium heat,
20–25 minutes, or until rice is tender and liquid starts to thicken.
Shred the cooled chicken by removing the skin and tearing the meat
into bite-sized pieces, discarding the bones and skin. You should
have about 3 cups of shredded meat.
Stir bok choy and shredded chicken into the soup, and simmer
for 2–3 minutes, or until bok choy is slightly softened.
Season with salt and pepper to taste.
Serve bowls of this soup with little side bowls of sliced
red chilies, julienned ginger and chopped cilantro for garnishing,
if using.

Who needs to go to the doctor when you can make this healthy and healing soup!

Nick's
AVGOLEMONO SOUP

We've been eating at the Main Street Diner for 40 years! The food is always so perfect,
the service is top notch, and the love you feel in this restaurant is like being part of the Diner and Diamond family.
Thanks Con, Nick and everyone at the Diner for sharing your fabulous avgolemono soup with us! • SERVES 4–6

INGREDIENTS

¼ cup butter
1 large onion, diced
6 cups chicken stock
2 cups converted white rice
2 egg yolks, room temperature
¼ cup freshly squeezed lemon juice,
    plus more for finishing
    (about 2 lemons in total)
1 tbsp flour
sea salt and freshly ground pepper
parsley or dill, for garnish
2 tbsp extra-virgin olive oil

METHOD

Melt butter in a large stock pot over medium heat,
then sauté onion until softened.
Add chicken stock and bring to a boil.
Add rice and simmer for 2 minutes.
Whisk egg yolks in a mixing bowl using an electric mixer
on medium-low speed until well beaten and fluffy.
Whisk in lemon juice, then add flour and whisk
just to combine.
Whisk 1 cup hot stock mixture into the yolk and lemon
mixture until smooth.
Whisk yolk mixture into the hot chicken stock.
Season with salt and pepper to taste.
Serve in soup bowls and garnish with parsley or dill,
another squeeze of lemon and a drizzle of olive oil.

*Adding the hot liquid to the egg yolk mixture ensures
that the soup doesn't get lumpy when adding the eggs.*

Go to the Diner and eat this soup and remember to thank the team for sharing their old family recipe with us!

FRENCH ONION SOUP

The Hume Hotel in Nelson is the coziest place to go on a snowy day. We recommend having a bowl of their French onion soup in the Library Lounge. Thanks to Shawn Trainor and Ryan Martin and the whole Hume team for creating such a haven for us Nelsonites, and for this delicious bowl of soup. • SERVES 6–8

INGREDIENTS

¼ cup olive oil

¼ cup butter

5 red onions, halved lengthwise
   and thinly sliced

2 white onions, halved lengthwise
   and thinly sliced

5 shallots, halved lengthwise
   and thinly sliced

4 garlic cloves, minced

4 bay leaves

1 tbsp sea salt, plus more as needed

2 tbsp brown sugar

1 cup cognac (St-Rémy or Hennessy)

1 cup white wine

8 cups beef stock

1 tbsp Worcestershire sauce

¼ cup fresh thyme, chopped

½ tsp hot sauce, such as Tabasco

freshly ground pepper

4–6 slices sourdough bread

2 cups Gruyère, grated

METHOD

Place oil and butter in a large, heavy-bottomed pot over medium-high heat.

Add onions, shallots, garlic, bay leaves and salt.

Cook at medium-high for 20 minutes, stirring occasionally.

Stir in brown sugar and turn down heat to low. Simmer for 1–1½ hours, or until onions are caramelized, stirring occasionally.

Stir in cognac and wine and simmer for 10 minutes or until the liquid has cooked into the onions.

Add beef stock, Worcestershire, thyme and Tabasco and stir.

Simmer for 20–30 minutes.

Season with salt and pepper to taste.

TO ASSEMBLE

Preheat oven to broil.

Toast sourdough slices in a toaster and set aside.

Ladle soup into individual ovenproof soup bowls and place on a foil-lined baking sheet.

Top each bowl of soup with a piece of sourdough, trimming bread as needed.

Distribute Gruyère evenly over the bread.

Place the pan on the middle rack of the oven and broil until the cheese is melted, bubbly and golden brown.

Ryan Martin of the Hume Hotel told us he reads *Whitewater Cooks* recipes to his sons as bedtime stories. We hope his little boys fall off to a deep sleep while he's reading this recipe to them!

Sarah's GREEN SOUP
with Gnocchi Dumplings

Sarah made this healthy green soup for Conner when he was under the weather one day this winter.
He was healed! • SERVES 4–6

INGREDIENTS

2 tbsp olive oil
1 bulb fennel, finely diced
1 yellow onion, finely diced
4 cloves garlic, minced
2 stalks celery, sliced on the bias
4 cups vegetable stock
sea salt and freshly ground pepper
4 cups loosely packed spinach
1 cup loosely packed basil
1 9-oz package fresh gnocchi
1½ cups green peas, fresh or frozen
1 13-oz can white beans, drained and rinsed
1 lemon, juice of
2 cups Parmesan, finely grated, divided

METHOD

Heat olive oil in a large pot over medium-high heat.
Add fennel, onion, garlic and celery. Sauté for 7–8 minutes, or until softened and golden.
Add vegetable stock. Season with salt and pepper to taste.
Bring to a boil, then reduce to a simmer. Cover and simmer for 10 minutes.
Blanch spinach and basil while the soup simmers.
To do so, prepare and set aside a bowl of ice water, and then pour boiling water from a kettle over the greens in a pot. Almost immediately, once spinach and basil are softened, shock them in the ice water and let sit for a minute or two until the water is cool.
Strain the blanched greens and blend with an immersion stick until very smooth. Set aside.
Add gnocchi, peas, beans and lemon juice to the stock mixture.
Increase heat to bring the stock mixture to a gentle boil and cook gnocchi about 2–3 minutes.
Reduce heat to low, and stir in the blended greens and half the Parmesan.
Serve hot with a generous garnish of Parmesan (as much as your heart desires!) and a crack of pepper.

The packaged gnocchi can be replaced with cubed yellow potatoes —
you'll just need to let them cook for a while longer until they're fork tender.

Rainy Day Indian-Spiced
TOMATO SOUP

We love a spicy bowl of this Indian-spiced curried tomato soup.
It's just what you need on a rainy day in Vancouver. • SERVES 4–6

INGREDIENTS

⅓ cup olive oil
1 medium yellow onion, diced
sea salt and freshly ground pepper
2 tsp ground turmeric
1 tsp ground cayenne
   (or more or less depending on your taste)
2 tbsp black mustard seeds
2 cups vegetable or chicken stock
1 28-oz can tomatoes, puréed
2 cups yellow potatoes
   chopped into ½-inch cubes
1 13-oz can coconut milk
4 cups loosely packed fresh spinach leaves
2–3 pappadums per person

METHOD

Heat oil in a medium-sized pot
over medium heat.
Sauté diced onion for 4–5 minutes,
or until translucent.
Season with salt and pepper to taste, add spices,
and cook for 2–3 minutes, or until fragrant.
Stir in stock and tomatoes, and bring to a simmer.
Add potatoes and simmer for 15–20 minutes,
or until tender.
Mix in coconut milk until incorporated and
return to a simmer.
Add spinach just before serving and
serve 1 or 2 pappadums with each bowl.

This tomato soup would pair well with
a mango chutney grilled cheese sandwich and a side of raita.

ROASTED CARROTS
with Whipped Sumac Feta

Roasted carrots are truly the perfect vessel for different spices and flavour combinations.
Here we nestle them on a bed of amazing whipped sumac feta and sprinkle them with pistachios and
pomegranates for a beautiful and delicious dish. • SERVES 4

INGREDIENTS

Roasted Carrots

10–12 medium-sized rainbow or regular carrots,
  cleaned with a vegetable brush, not peeled
  (whole or sliced lengthwise for uniform size)
3 tbsp extra-virgin olive oil
2 tbsp honey
½–1 tsp red chili Ûakes
½ tsp cumin
½ tsp smoked paprika
⅛ tsp cinnamon
1 tsp za'atar
sea salt and freshly ground pepper
¼ cup pistachios, roughly chopped, for garnish
parsley, mint or cilantro, chopped, for garnish
¼ cup pomegranate seeds, for garnish (optional)

Whipped Sumac Feta

½ cup feta
½ cup full-fat Greek yogurt
1 tbsp extra-virgin olive oil
1 tsp freshly squeezed lemon juice
1 tsp ground sumac

METHOD

Roasted Carrots

Preheat oven to 425°F.
Grease a baking tray with olive oil and place carrots on it.
Drizzle carrots with olive oil and honey, sprinkle with
all the spices, and toss to evenly coat.
Arrange carrots in a single layer on the tray.
Roast for 20–30 minutes, or until fork tender and
caramelized, tossing halfway through the cooking time.

Whipped Sumac Feta

Process all ingredients in a food processor until
well combined.

TO SERVE

Serve carrots on a bed of the whipped feta, and garnish
with pistachios, herbs and pomegranate seeds, if using.

*It's important to have carrots that are the same size
for this recipe. Leave them whole if small in diameter
or slice lengthwise if they're bigger.*

Sumac is a Middle Eastern spice with a tart, lemony flavour
and the most beautiful deep-red colour. It's just heavenly in this whipped feta.

SALADS

◆

◆

THE GREENK
Salad

Everybody knows and loves the famous Greek salad, but whenever we've visited Greece we've heard from the locals that they more frequently make a version of this green salad as their daily house salad. It's got the same herby feta combination that we love in Greek salad, but comes together in half the time! Conner created this salad and in our family we affectionately call it the Greenk. • SERVES 4–6

INGREDIENTS

¼ cup extra-virgin olive oil
1 lemon, juice of
½ tsp dried oregano
sea salt and freshly ground pepper
1 head romaine lettuce, washed and torn
   or chopped into bite sized pieces
1 cup feta, crumbled
1 bunch dill, chopped
   (about 1 cup loosely packed)
1 bunch fresh mint, chopped
   (about 1 cup loosely packed)
½ cup Italian parsley, chopped
2 green onions, thinly sliced on the bias
4 Persian cucumbers, peeled into ribbons

METHOD

Whisk olive oil, lemon juice, and oregano
in a small bowl.
Season with salt and pepper to taste.
Place the romaine in a large, shallow salad bowl.
Top with feta, herbs, green onions and cucumber.
Drizzle the dressing over and toss gently when
ready to serve.

Conner named this salad the Greek because it's a combination of a Greek
and a green salad! We love to add chopped pistachios if we have some on hand.

SHAVED FENNEL and PECORINO
Salad

Fennel and olives are a fantastic combination! This yummy salad is the perfect side for your favourite grilled fresh fish or the Swordfish with Pan Piccata Sauce (page 120). Use a mandoline if you have one, but be careful! • SERVES 4

INGREDIENTS

2 medium bulbs fennel,
  shaved on a mandoline or thinly sliced
3 stalks celery,
  shaved on a mandoline or thinly sliced
1 tbsp champagne vinegar
¼ cup extra-virgin olive oil
½ tbsp honey
sea salt and freshly ground pepper
⅓ cup Castelvetrano or similar green olives,
  smashed or coarsely chopped
½ cup pecorino, crumbled or grated
2 tbsp Italian parsley, finely chopped

METHOD

Place the fennel and celery in a large bowl.
Whisk vinegar, oil and honey in a small bowl. Pour over fennel and celery mixture and toss.
Season with salt and a generous crack of pepper to taste.
Set aside the seasoned fennel and celery to marinate in the bowl for 15–30 minutes.

TO SERVE

Arrange the fennel and celery on a rimmed plate.
Top with olives, pecorino and parsley.

A handful of coarsely chopped Medjool dates is a great addition to this salad.

SEDONA
Salad

We first made this fabulous salad when on a hiking trip in Sedona. It was hearty enough to eat for lunch and kept us going all afternoon. We loved how the slightly crunchy quinoa added to all the other textures. The chipotle dressing and Southwest flavours will make you feel like you're in Sedona too! • SERVES 4

INGREDIENTS

Dressing

3 tbsp apple cider vinegar
2 tbsp agave syrup
2 chipotle peppers in adobo sauce,
    finely chopped (about 2 tbsp)
½ tsp sea salt
½ tsp freshly ground pepper
½ tsp dried oregano
10–12 fresh basil leaves
¼ cup extra-virgin olive oil
¼ cup avocado or other neutral oil

Salad

1 cup cooked quinoa,
    prepared to package instructions
2 tbsp extra-virgin olive oil
1 tsp sea salt, divided
1 cup corn niblets, cooked and drained
2 tsp tajin (optional), or 1 tsp chili powder
freshly ground pepper
1 bunch lacinato kale, torn into bite-sized pieces
1 head romaine, torn into bite-sized pieces
1 cup jicama or radishes, ¼-inch-diced
1 15-oz can black beans, drained and rinsed
2 cups cherry tomatoes, halved
2 avocados, diced
½ cup cotija or feta, finely crumbled, divided

METHOD

Dressing

Blend all ingredients in a food processor until smooth.

Salad

Preheat oven to 375°F.
Mix cooked quinoa, oil and ½ tsp salt.
Spread quinoa mixture evenly on a baking sheet.
Bake for 25–30 minutes, tossing after 15 minutes, or until it starts to crisp up. Set aside.
Mix corn with tajin and season with the remaining ½ tsp salt and pepper to taste.
Toss kale and lettuce in a large bowl.
Top with corn mixture, jicama, beans, tomatoes, avocados, quinoa and ¼ cup cotija.
Pour dressing over and toss to coat all ingredients.
Serve portions garnished with the remaining cotija.

Tajin is a Mexican spice blend
with the flavours of chili, salt and lime.

This is a great salad to take to your next potluck or picnic!

HALE HOUSE
Salad

Hale means house in the Hawaiian language, so this salad's name is a bit redundant.
There's a place on Maui that serves this perfect salad alongside thin-crust pizzas — you should too!
Make sure everyone gets a good hunk of goat cheese.   •   SERVES 4–6

INGREDIENTS

Dressing

¼ cup champagne or sherry vinegar
1 orange, juice of
1 small shallot, finely chopped
1 1-inch piece ginger, peeled and finely grated
1 garlic clove, minced
½ tsp ground cardamom
¼ tsp crushed red pepper flakes
2 tbsp sesame seeds, toasted
1 tsp honey
1 tsp tamari or soy sauce
sea salt and freshly ground pepper
½ cup extra-virgin olive oil

Salad

1 head romaine lettuce, torn into
   bite-sized pieces, or 8 cups spring greens
1 cup alfalfa sprouts
4 medium carrots, peeled and grated
4 oz goat cheese, crumbled
   or broken into large chunks

METHOD

Put all dressing ingredients except oil in a bowl
and whisk to mix.
Slowly whisk in oil until well blended.
Place romaine or spring greens in a large salad bowl.
Pour dressing over and toss.
Top with sprouts, carrots and cheese, and serve.

Adding a piece of grilled mahi mahi or some grilled shrimp to this salad would be amazing!

Emmy's MISO-GRILLED CHICKEN
and Crunchy Vegetable Salad

Emmy made this salad for dinner with some girlfriends on a hot evening on the lake last summer. It was light, flavourful and just what they needed to get their protein and fresh veggies, and, most importantly, quality girl time together! • SERVES 4

INGREDIENTS

Dressing

½ cup plus 1 tbsp white miso paste
½ cup plus 1 tbsp warm water
¼ cup sesame oil
3 tbsp rice wine vinegar
1 tbsp soy sauce
2 tsp dark brown sugar
1 1-inch piece ginger, peeled and grated
1½ tsp garlic, minced

Salad

1 cup quinoa, rinsed
1¾ cups water
4 boneless, skinless chicken breasts
1 cup carrots, shredded
1 cup red cabbage, shredded
1 cup red pepper, julienned
¼ cup green onions, thinly sliced
¼ cup cilantro leaves, loosely packed
1 cup snap peas, halved and blanched
2 cups edamame, cooked according
   to package instructions
2 cups spinach leaves, loosely packed
sea salt and freshly ground pepper
4 tsp sesame seeds, toasted

METHOD

Dressing

Whisk all ingredients in a medium-sized bowl until blended. Set aside.

Salad

Preheat barbecue to medium-high heat.
Put quinoa in a medium pot and pour in water. Bring to a boil, cover, reduce the heat and simmer for 15 minutes.
Remove from the heat and let sit, covered, for 10 minutes. Fluff with a fork.

Pour 4 tbsp of the dressing into a small bowl. Brush chicken breasts with dressing and grill for 6–8 minutes per side, or until just cooked through, being careful not to overcook. Discard any remaining dressing that was used on the chicken.
Toss carrot, cabbage, red pepper, green onions and cilantro in a large bowl and set aside.
Divide quinoa among four individual serving bowls.
Place a little pile of the carrot and cabbage mixture, snap peas, edamame and spinach leaves on the quinoa. Season with salt and pepper to taste.
Top with the sliced chicken and sprinkle with sesame seeds.
Drizzle with the remainder of the yummy miso dressing and dive in!

Feel free to just toss all the salad ingredients together in a big bowl instead of composing them into individual serving bowls. This salad would also be absolutely fabulous with grilled salmon fillets!

CUCUMBER SALAD

When in Venice Beach, we always have to go to our favourite Italian café for lunch.
They serve the best, healthiest and freshest food, and the ambience is just so California hip!
This is our version of the cucumber salad they serve there. • SERVES 4–6

INGREDIENTS

1 red onion, sliced thinly along the grain
½ cup cider vinegar
2 lemons, zest and juice of, divided
3 tbsp honey
1 cup water
1 tsp salt
10–12 Persian cucumbers,
    chopped into asymmetrical bite-sized pieces
2 tbsp za'atar
1 tsp crushed red pepper flakes
¼ cup extra-virgin olive oil
sea salt and freshly ground pepper
½ cup mint leaves, loosely packed,
    julienned, divided
¾ cup feta, crumbled

METHOD

Place sliced onion in a clean jar.
Put vinegar, juice of 1 lemon, honey, water and salt in a small saucepan and bring to a boil. Immediately remove from heat.
Pour the heated mixture into the jar and push the onion down to submerge completely. Set aside for 30 minutes, after which the pickled onion should be perfect.
Mix cucumbers, za'atar, pepper flakes, the remaining lemon juice, all the zest and oil. Season with salt and pepper to taste.
Add half the mint and toss well.

TO SERVE

Place cucumber mixture on a platter, then top with half the pickled onion, feta, and the remaining mint.
Sprinkle on more pepper flakes, za'atar, salt and pepper, if desired.

*Slicing an onion along the grain refers to halving it from the root to stem end, and then slicing
in the same direction. This technique preserves the fibres and maintains the pickled onion's texture.
Cover the rest of the pickled onion and save in the fridge for up to two weeks — you'll find a good use for it!*

When in Venice Beach, go to Muscle Beach, the skate park and as many restaurants as possible!

BURRATA and FARRO SALAD
with Roasted Cherry Tomatoes

We love farro, burrata and wilted greens, so what could possibly be better than eating these three different textures in one Mediterranean-inspired salad! Farro is the traditional grain of the Mediterranean. In France it's called épeautre, which is the French word for spelt. We have so many memories of eating salads just like this all over Italy and France. It's a perfect accompaniment to grilled fish or roasted chicken for dinner, but also a lovely and hearty lunch salad all on its own. • SERVES 4

INGREDIENTS

Pesto • *Makes about 1 cup*

2 cups fresh basil leaves, loosely packed,
  rinsed and dried
½ tsp Maldon or coarse salt
1 large garlic clove, minced
2 tbsp pine nuts or walnuts
½ cup extra-virgin olive oil, divided
½ cup Parmesan, freshly grated

Salad

1 cup farro, cooked according to package instructions
4 cups cherry tomatoes
1 red onion, peeled, quartered and
  cut into 1-inch wedges
4 tbsp extra-virgin olive oil, divided,
  plus more as needed
Maldon salt and freshly ground pepper
½ tsp crushed red pepper flakes
½ cup pesto, homemade or store-bought,
  plus more to taste
1 lemon, zest and juice of
2 cups arugula, baby kale or spinach (they're all good!)
2 4-oz balls fresh burrata, torn into bite-sized pieces,
  or ½ cup crumbled feta
¼ cup fresh basil or Italian parsley, roughly chopped,
  for garnish

METHOD

Pesto

Blend basil, salt, garlic, nuts, and about half the oil in a food processor or blender until just smooth.
Pour in the remaining oil and blend until smooth.
Stir in Parmesan.

Salad

Preheat oven to 400°F.
Place cooked and drained farro in a large salad bowl.
Mix tomatoes and onion with 2 tablespoons oil on a parchment-lined baking sheet and toss until everything is coated, then season with salt, pepper and red pepper flakes.
Roast for 30–40 minutes, or until tomatoes blister.
Toss the farro with the remaining 2 tablespoons oil, then mix in pesto.
Scrape the warm onion, tomatoes, and their juices from the baking sheet into the farro mixture and toss.
Add lemon zest and juice, then stir in your choice of greens and let them wilt slightly.
Season with salt and pepper to taste and stir in more pesto if desired.
Season burrata with salt, pepper and oil to taste, if desired, and place on the salad.
Garnish with basil or parsley.
Serve a big scoop of salad with a piece of burrata for each person.

We often use store-bought pesto for this salad because there are so many good organic ones in stores these days.

Sheri's Honey Lime
BAJA SLAW

This versatile coleslaw is great on fish tacos and with our Chicken Enchiladas (page 126).
Sheri says she often has this slaw ready to go in her fridge since it pairs well with so many things.
Thanks again, Sheri! • SERVES 4–6

INGREDIENTS

2 tsp lime zest
2 limes, juice of (about ¼ cup)
2 tbsp honey
1 garlic clove, minced
½ tsp sea salt
¼ tsp freshly ground pepper
¼ tsp crushed red pepper Ûakes
3 tbsp neutral oil, such as canola or avocado
1 small head red cabbage,
  sliced as thinly as possible
2 medium carrots, grated
2 green onions, thinly sliced
½ cup cilantro, chopped, for garnish

METHOD

Whisk lime zest and juice, honey, garlic, salt, pepper and pepper flakes in a small bowl.
Whisk in oil gradually until well blended.
Mix cabbage, carrots and green onions in a large bowl and toss with lime honey vinaigrette to lightly coat.
Refrigerate, covered, for 2 hours.
Sprinkle with cilantro and serve.

You can add just about any crunchy vegetable to this coleslaw!
We've used fennel, celery and daikon.

Venetian

BRUSSELS SPROUTS SALAD

Taking the time to slice the Brussels sprouts super thin is worth the effort here — it really makes a difference!
We first tried this at an amazing Italian restaurant near Conner's house in Venice Beach and knew we had
to create a Whitewater Cooks version to share. • SERVES 4

INGREDIENTS

Salad

1 lb Brussels sprouts, shaved on a mandoline
 (about 5 cups)
2 cups red grapes, halved lengthwise
½ cup Marcona almonds, roughly chopped
½ cup pecorino, crumbled or grated
⅓ cup Parmesan, grated

Dressing

2 tbsp shallot, minced
2 tbsp red wine vinegar
1 lemon, juice of
1 tsp honey
½ cup extra-virgin olive oil
sea salt and freshly ground pepper

METHOD

Salad

Toss all ingredients in a large salad bowl
and set aside.

Dressing

Whisk shallot, vinegar, lemon juice
and honey in a small bowl.
Pour oil in in a steady stream,
whisking to blend.
Season with salt and pepper to taste.
Pour dressing over the salad and toss so
you get all the flavours in every bite.

When it comes to the Brussels sprouts,
the thinner the better for this salad.
It's worth the effort to shave them on a mandoline!

We really love the grapes, Marcona almonds and Parmesan in this Brussels sprouts salad.
It's a perfect combination of sweet and salty.

BC

LOUIE

This British Columbian version of the California classic Shrimp Louie doesn't ask you to choose between shrimp or crab — you get both! The dressing is also much lighter than the classic, making it a healthier version. The result is like a coastal niçoise salad. It's a perfect summertime lunch! • SERVES 4–6

INGREDIENTS

Dressing

½ cup plain Greek yogurt
¼ cup ketchup
1 dill pickle, finely diced (about ¼ cup)
1 stalk celery, finely diced (about ¼ cup)
1 clove garlic, minced
2 tsp dried dill
1½ tsp horseradish
½ lemon, juice of
1 tsp paprika
4 dashes hot sauce, such as Tabasco (optional)
sea salt and freshly ground pepper

Salad

1 lb jumbo shrimp (18/24 count)
4 medium eggs, boiled for 7–7½ minutes
  and cooled in cold water
1 head romaine, washed and chopped into
  bite-sized pieces
8–12 asparagus spears, blanched and cooled
1 cup cherry tomatoes, halved
1 medium avocado, cubed
½ cup cooked Dungeness crab meat
½ lemon, cut into wedges
sea salt and freshly ground pepper

METHOD

Dressing

Mix all ingredients in a small bowl and set aside.

Salad

Bring to a boil a large pot of salted water. Add shrimp and cook for about 4 minutes, or until they are pink and cooked all the way through.

Drop shrimp into an ice bath. Remove with a slotted spoon and set aside to dry.

Peel eggs and cut into quarters lengthwise.

Assemble the salad by creating a bed of romaine on a large platter and setting piles of asparagus, shrimp, eggs, tomatoes, avocado, crab meat and lemon wedges over it.

Season the salad with salt and pepper to taste.

Serve with a bowl of the dressing on the side.

Each person can serve themselves with a little bit of everything,
adding spoonfuls of the dressing to their own taste. So delicious, so classic!

MINTY PEAS and PROSCIUTTO SALAD

with Perfect Ricotta Dressing

This recipe includes our new favourite salad dressing in the world! It's so creamy, light, and perfectly balanced. When you make it, you'll agree! • SERVES 6–8

INGREDIENTS

Dressing

½ cup ricotta
¾ tsp sea salt
1 medium shallot, finely diced
1 clove garlic, finely minced
1 tsp granulated sugar or honey
¼ cup champagne or sherry vinegar
¾ cup extra-virgin olive oil
sea salt and freshly cracked pepper

Salad

1 head butter lettuce, washed well
  and torn into bite-sized pieces
1 head radicchio, washed well
  and torn into bite-sized pieces
1½ cups microgreens,
  or micro alfalfa or pea shoots
sea salt and freshly ground pepper
1½ cups green peas, blanched
6–8 basil leaves, torn into small pieces
6–8 mint leaves, torn into small pieces
12 thin slices prosciutto

METHOD

Dressing

Whisk ricotta with 1 tbsp water and ¾ tsp salt
in a medium-sized bowl.
Rinse shallot under cold water in a strainer to make
the flavour more mild, and drain.
Add shallot, garlic, sugar and vinegar to ricotta mixture
and whisk.
Pour in oil slowly while whisking to incorporate.
Season with salt and pepper to taste.

Salad

Toss lettuce, radicchio and microgreens in a large bowl and
season lightly with salt and pepper to taste.
Mix peas with basil and mint in a separate bowl and
season with salt and pepper to taste.
Pour the dressing over the greens and toss to lightly coat.
Serve the greens in a tall pile, using layers of prosciutto to
build it up and topping each layer with a handful
of the herby peas.

Conner ate a version of this salad in New York City and has never forgotten it!

DINNERS

◆

◆

CHICKEN CHILI

with Black Beans and Pickled Onions

Shelley wishes she'd had this chicken chili recipe when she ran the Fresh Tracks Café at the Whitewater Ski Resort, because the skiers would have gone crazy for it! The cabbage and pickled onions really set it apart from regular chili. • SERVES 6

INGREDIENTS

1 yellow onion, quartered
1 poblano pepper, roughly chopped into chunks
2 jalapenos, roughly chopped (de-seed them
    if your spice tolerance is low)
2 celery stalks, roughly chopped
8 boneless, skinless chicken thighs,
    chopped into 1-inch cubes
sea salt and freshly ground pepper
4 tbsp olive oil
1 tbsp ground cumin
½ tbsp paprika
½ tbsp chili powder
4 cups chicken stock
1 red onion, halved lengthwise and
    thinly sliced along the grain
½ cup apple cider vinegar
½ orange, juice of (¼ cup)
3 tbsp honey
1 small head white cabbage, shredded
    (about 2 cups)
2 14-oz cans black beans, drained and rinsed
1 cup sour cream, for garnish
½ bunch cilantro leaves, for garnish
2 green onions, thinly sliced on the bias,
    for garnish

The Mexican Street Corn recipe (page 32)
would be muy bueno with this chicken chili.

METHOD

Pulse yellow onion, peppers and celery in a food processor until finely chopped, to make a sofrito.

Season chopped chicken thighs with salt and pepper to taste.

Heat oil over medium heat in a large stock pot. Add chicken and brown evenly on all sides.

Remove chicken from oil and set aside.

Add sofrito to the pot with the oil and rendered chicken fat, and cook for 3–4 minutes, stirring frequently.

Add spices and cook for an additional 3–4 minutes to allow the flavours to bloom.

Return chicken to the pot and add stock. Bring to a gentle boil and cook for 20 minutes.

Place red onion in a very clean jar.

Heat vinegar, orange juice, honey and 1 cup water to a boil in a small saucepan and immediately remove from heat.

Pour the heated mixture into the jar and push the onion down to submerge completely. Set aside for 30 minutes, allowing onion to pickle.

Add shredded cabbage to the chicken and stock after 20 minutes of cooking and cook 20 minutes more.

Stir in beans, let them heat for a few minutes and remove from heat.

Serve the chili in bowls and garnish with sour cream, cilantro, green onions and pickled red onions.

A sofrito is a fragrant seasoning blend of various herbs, spices and vegetables, and is often used in Mexican cooking. • Slicing an onion along the grain refers to halving it from the root to stem end, and then slicing in the same direction. This technique preserves the fibres and maintains the pickled onion's texture.

CABERNET BRAISED SHORT RIBS
with Gorgonzola Polenta and Gremolata

Our friend Margie knows good wine and she knows great food. This recipe brings those two together and is always a huge hit. You can make the ribs, sauce and gremolata the day before and let the flavours meld while you wait! All you have to make the next day is the polenta. *Pronto* Margie! • SERVES 6–8

INGREDIENTS

Ribs

6–7 lbs meaty beef short ribs
2 tbsp fresh rosemary, finely chopped
2 tbsp fresh thyme, finely chopped
1 tbsp kosher salt
1 tbsp pepper
2 tbsp neutral oil, such as canola or avocado, plus more if needed
1 bottle Cabernet Sauvignon
3 cups beef broth
2 tbsp butter, room temperature
2 tbsp flour

Gorgonzola Polenta

5 cups chicken broth
1 cup coarse cornmeal
½ cup Gorgonzola, crumbled
⅓ cup whipping cream

Gremolata

¼ cup Italian parsley, finely chopped
2 lemons, zest of (about 3 tbsp)
2 garlic cloves, minced
1½ tbsp fresh rosemary, finely chopped
1½ tbsp fresh thyme, finely chopped

METHOD

Ribs

Place ribs in one layer in a glass baking dish.
Mix rosemary, thyme, salt and pepper and sprinkle all over. Cover and refrigerate overnight..
Let stand at room temperature for 1 hour.
Preheat oven to 350°F.
Heat oil in a Dutch oven or heavy-bottomed ovenproof pot over medium-high heat. Sear ribs in batches for about 8 minutes per batch, or until browned on all sides, adding more oil if needed.
Transfer ribs to a large bowl or platter.
Pour off the fat from the pot and discard. Add wine and beef broth and bring to a simmer, scraping up any browned bits. Return ribs and accumulated juices to the pot. Bring to a boil.
Cover pot, place in the pre-heated oven and braise for about 2–2½ hours, or until meat is very tender and almost falling off the bone.
Remove ribs from braising liquid, place in an ovenproof baking dish, and cover tightly. If serving tonight, keep warm in a 225°F oven.
Cool the braising liquid until the fat starts to rise to the top. You can put the pot in the fridge to speed up the process.
Skim all fat from the top of the liquid with a slotted spoon, then boil for about 20 minutes, or until reduced to about 3 cups.

Blend butter and flour well with a fork in a small bowl. Add to the reduced braising liquid and whisk over medium-high heat for about 2 minutes, or until the sauce thickens slightly.
If you're planning to serve this dish the next day, you're done for now! Put everything in containers, cool, and then cover and refrigerate. Before serving, put the ribs in an ovenproof dish covered with tinfoil. Heat in a 225°F oven for 30 minutes and warm the sauce up on the stove.

Gorgonzola Polenta

Heat chicken broth to a boil in a heavy-bottomed pot.
Pour in cornmeal gradually, whisking constantly.
Return mixture to a boil. Reduce heat to low, and cover and simmer for about 10–12 minutes, or until polenta is tender, stirring often.
Remove from heat and add Gorgonzola and cream. Stir until cheese is melted and season with salt and pepper to taste.

Gremolata

Mix all ingredients in a small bowl.
Cover and chill until needed.

TO SERVE

Distribute polenta among serving plates or large bowls.
Top with ribs and a spoonful of sauce.
Sprinkle with gremolata and serve.

Your favourite butcher will have the best beef short ribs!

Sweet Potato Thai Green Curry
with PAPPADUM-CRUSTED HALIBUT

Conner's wife, Sarah, is vegetarian and Conner created this perfectly fabulous Thai curry just for her. It includes a homemade green curry paste. We added the pappadum-crusted halibut and it really is a match made in heaven! • SERVES 4

INGREDIENTS

Green Curry Paste

1 tbsp coriander seeds, toasted
½ tbsp cumin seeds, toasted
2 large shallots, diced
3 cloves garlic, minced
1 1-inch piece ginger or galangal,
   if available, peeled and grated
1 lime leaf
2 bird's eye or Thai chilis, sliced
   (vary the amount depending on
   your spice tolerance)
1 bunch cilantro, stems only
1 tbsp neutral oil,
   such as canola or avocado

Curry

2 tbsp canola or avocado oil
sea salt and freshly ground pepper
2 large sweet potatoes, peeled
   and diced into ½-inch cubes
2 13-oz cans coconut milk
1 tsp fish sauce (optional)
½ tbsp palm sugar or light brown sugar
1 stalk lemongrass, halved crosswise
10 leaves Thai or regular basil,
   roughly chopped
1 lime, juice of
2 cups kale, swiss chard, or spinach, de-
   stemmed and torn into bite-sized pieces
2 cups uncooked rice or quinoa, prepared
   according to package instructions

Halibut

¼ cup butter, room temperature
2 cloves garlic, minced
½ lime, zest and juice of,
   plus 1 lime, sliced for garnish
4 4-inch pappadums
4 6-oz skinless halibut fillets
sea salt and
   freshly ground pepper

METHOD

Green Curry Paste

Purée all ingredients in a food processor.

Curry

Heat oil in a large pot over medium-high heat. Add green curry paste and sauté. Stir frequently for 3–5 minutes, or until fragrant. Season with salt and pepper to taste.
Mix in sweet potato and sauté 3–5 minutes more.
Pour in coconut milk, then add fish sauce, if using, sugar, lemongrass and basil.
Bring to a boil, then reduce heat to a simmer. Cook for about 20 minutes, or until sauce reaches desired consistency and sweet potato is cooked through.
Remove the lemongrass and discard.
Stir in lime juice and leafy greens. Let curry sit for about 10 minutes to allow the flavours to settle and the greens to soften.

Halibut

Preheat oven to 400°F.
Whip butter, garlic and lime zest and juice in a small bowl.
Toast pappadums in the oven or a frying pan over medium-high heat with 1 tbsp oil. Flip once golden brown. Process in a food processor until just crumbly.
Place halibut on a parchment-lined pan. Sprinkle with salt and pepper to taste, then spread with the whipped butter. Press on the pappadum crumbs to create a nice crust.
Bake for 12–15 minutes, or until just cooked through and the crust browned.

TO SERVE

Place rice on a dinner plate and spoon on curry.
Place halibut on the rice and curry, and garnish with a lime slice.

If making your own curry paste is too daunting, use a 4-ounce jar of green curry paste instead.
The curry alone is hearty enough for dinner, so you could please the vegetarians and fish eaters at your table!

Greek
FEAST

Conner came up with the idea to make a simple little Greek feast that can be prepared in less than an hour.
Put on the Greek music and get in the mood! • SERVES 4

INGREDIENTS

1½ cups plain full-fat Greek yogurt
2 cloves garlic, grated on a microplane
1 lemon, juice of
sea salt and freshly ground pepper
12 lamb loin chops
3 Persian cucumbers, diced
2 large heirloom tomatoes, diced (about 3 cups)
2 red bell peppers, diced
¼ red onion, diced
1 cup feta, crumbled
¾ cup pitted kalamata olives
½ cup fresh mint, chopped
4 tbsp extra-virgin olive oil
4–6 pita breads
1 cup hummus, store-bought or homemade

METHOD

Preheat oven to 400°F.

Mix yogurt, garlic and lemon juice in a large bowl
and season with salt and pepper to taste.

Transfer half the yogurt mixture to another large bowl.

Add lamb and coat chops in the yogurt mixture.
Set aside.

Stir cucumbers, tomatoes, peppers and onion into the
yogurt remaining in the other bowl to coat. Mix in
feta, olives and mint, and set this Greek salad aside.

Heat oil over medium-high heat in a cast-iron pan and
work in batches to sear chops for 3 minutes per side.

Return all lamb chops to the pan and roast in the oven
for 10 minutes.

Wrap pita bread in tinfoil and heat in the oven
for 5 minutes.

Serve lamb chops with the Greek salad, pita bread
and hummus.

You could, of course, grill the lamb chops and pita bread on the barbecue if your Greek feast is in the summertime.

Everyone's Favourite

ITALIAN SAUSAGE RIGATONI

Conner's friend Julia is the pasta queen! She made this for everyone when they were living together in West Hollywood. This recipe's called Everyone's Favourite because it truly is. It's been a favourite of Julia's family forever and her mom, Vic, taught her how to make it. • SERVES 4

INGREDIENTS

2 tbsp butter
½ yellow onion, šnely chopped
1 lb spicy Italian sausage, removed from casings
1 28-oz can whole peeled tomatoes
1 tbsp sea salt, plus more
freshly ground pepper
1 lb rigatoni pasta
¾ cup whole milk ricotta
½ cup basil leaves, julienned, divided
¾ cup Parmesan, finely grated, divided

METHOD

Melt butter in a heavy-bottomed pot over medium-high heat.

Add onion and cook until soft and golden brown.

Break up sausage meat in the pot and spread it out. Cook about 5 minutes, or until it starts to brown.

Add tomatoes (crushing them by hand) and their juices to the pot.

Season with salt and pepper to taste, keeping in mind the sausage is already seasoned.

Reduce the sauce for 15–20 minutes over medium-low heat.

Bring to a boil 4 quarts water in a large pot while the sauce reduces and add 1 tbsp salt.

Cook rigatoni to just shy of al dente.

Reserve 1–2 cups of the pasta water before straining.

Increase heat to medium for the sauce and add ricotta and half the basil.

Stir in the cooked pasta and half the Parmesan.

Add ½ cup of the reserved pasta water to bring everything together, and cook for an additional 2 minutes. Add more pasta water as desired to get the consistency just right.

Serve hot with the remaining basil and Parmesan for garnish.

This will become your family's favourite pasta sauce, just like it is for Julia's!

THE FOOD WE LOVE

104

WHITEWATER COOKS

DINNERS

DOUBLE FENNEL
Pork Chops

This is an easy mid-week dinner with tons of flavour. It includes an amazing, spicy and herbaceous condiment, zhug, that goes well with so many dishes. The recipe for this Middle-Eastern sauce should leave you with leftovers to use with different meals throughout the week. Make sure to use thick-cut pork chops! • SERVES 2–4

INGREDIENTS

Zhug
1½ tsp freshly ground pepper
1½ tsp ground coriander
1 tsp ground cumin
¼ tsp ground cardamom
6 garlic cloves, crushed
4 serrano peppers, roughly chopped
   (remove the seeds if your spice tolerance is low)
2 bunches cilantro stems and leaves,
   roughly chopped (about 3 cups tightly packed)
1¼ bunches Italian parsley, leaves only,
   roughly chopped (about 1½ cups tightly packed)
½ cup extra-virgin olive oil
1 tsp kosher salt, or to taste

Pork Chops and Fennel
1½ tbsp ground fennel seeds
1 tsp ground coriander
2 tbsp brown sugar
3 tsp salt
1 tsp cracked pepper
2 bone-in thick pork chops, about 1 lb each
2 tbsp olive oil
2 bulbs fennel, sliced thinly

METHOD

Zhug

Pulse ground pepper, coriander, cumin, cardamom, garlic and peppers in a food processor until a paste forms.
Add herbs and continue to process until combined.
Pour in oil slowly while processing until well incorporated.
Add salt gradually to the mixture, tasting to get the balance just right.
Set aside the zhug.

Pork Chops and Fennel

Mix ground fennel seeds, coriander, sugar, and salt and pepper in a small bowl.
Rub pork chops all over with the mixture and let sit for an hour at room temperature. If you put the rub on the chops early in the day, refrigerate them and remove from the fridge an hour before cooking.
Heat oil in a large frying pan over medium-high heat.
Sear chops in hot oil on one side for 5–6 minutes.
Cook chops on the other side for 5–6 minutes, until just cooked through.
Set aside cooked chops on a plate, cover with tinfoil, and let rest.
Add sliced fennel to the pan with all the juices and fat from the pork chops and cook for 6–8 minutes, or until fennel is soft.

TO SERVE

Place a portion of the fennel on a plate.
Top with a chop and a generous spoonful of the zhug.

If you prefer to use whole spices in this recipe, feel free!
Just make sure to toast them until fragrant before grinding them with a mortar and pestle.

MARGIE'S CREAMY PRAWN LINGUINE
with Acorn Tomatoes and Kale

We got home from a long trip to Maui after delayed flights and a very snowy 10-hour drive back to Nelson.
The ever-thoughtful Margie had left the recipe and ingredients for this creamy and flavourful linguine on our counter.
We were so grateful and make it all the time now! • SERVES 4–6

INGREDIENTS

1 lb dried linguine
1 cup panko bread crumbs
2 tbsp parsley, chopped
1 tbsp extra-virgin olive oil
1 lb peeled and deveined prawns
sea salt and freshly ground pepper
4 tbsp butter
3 cloves garlic, minced
½ tsp crushed red pepper flakes
3 cups acorn or cherry tomatoes, halved
¼ cup white wine
1 cup whipping cream
1 lemon, juice of
½ cup Parmesan, grated
3 cups baby kale, chopped

METHOD

Cook linguine in a large pot of salted boiling water according to package directions until al dente.

Reserve ½ cup pasta water, drain pasta, and return to pot.

Brown panko in a large pan over medium-high heat, for about 5–8 minutes. Transfer to a small bowl, mix in parsley and set aside.

Heat oil in the pan over medium heat.

Add prawns and season with salt and pepper to taste.

Cook for about 4 minutes, or until prawns turn pink and cook through. Remove from the pan and set aside on a plate.

Add butter to the pan, and then add garlic and chili flakes and cook for about 1 minute, or until fragrant.

Add tomatoes to pan and cook for about 3 minutes, or until beginning to soften.

Season with a little more salt and pepper to taste.

Add wine and cook for about 5 minutes, or until mostly reduced.

Stir in cream, lemon juice and Parmesan.

Simmer for 4–5 minutes, or until the sauce is thickened.

Add pasta, prawns and kale and toss to coat, adding more pasta water if the sauce is too thick. Allow kale to wilt.

Serve each portion with a generous garnish of the parsley bread crumbs.

Open a bottle of Pinot Grigio from the Duhamel Store in Nelson and you're set!

Long-Roasted Lemony
LEG OF LAMB

Claire Hitchman is the most talented little cook and every time we eat dinner at her house we feel like we're
on a holiday in southern France or Greece! Here is her amazing slow-cooked lamb recipe. • SERVES 6–8

INGREDIENTS

5 lb bone-in leg of lamb
12 cloves garlic, divided
2 tbsp olive oil
sea salt and freshly ground pepper
3 tsp paprika
3 tsp garlic or onion powder
2 large onions, quartered
10 sprigs thyme
3 sprigs rosemary
3 tsp dried oregano
3 dried bay leaves or 5 fresh
2–3 lemons, juice of, plus more
1½ cups white wine
2 cups chicken stock
1 cup full-fat plain Greek yogurt
2 tsp preserved lemon, diced,
    or 1 lemon, zest of
fresh mint leaves for garnish

METHOD

Preheat the oven to 450°F.
Make about 25 incisions all over the lamb
but mostly on top with a small knife.
Slice 6 cloves garlic into slivers and stuff
them into the incisions.
Drizzle lamb with olive oil and
generously sprinkle and rub with salt,
pepper, paprika, and garlic powder.
Place lamb in a roasting pan and roast
for 30 minutes, or until it has a nice
brown crust.
Remove from the oven and turn heat
down to 350°F.
Turn lamb upside down.
Place all remaining ingredients except
yogurt and preserved lemon, and
including the remaining garlic, in the pan
around the lamb. Pour hot water into the
pan so it comes about a third of the way
up the lamb.
Cover the pan with a lid or parchment
paper and then 2 layers of foil.
Roast for 2½ hours, adding more water if
it dries out a bit.

Remove the pan from the oven and
uncover. Flip over the lamb leg.
Cover again and roast for a further
2½ hours, or until the meat is very tender.
Uncover and roast for a further
20–30 minutes, to brown.
Remove from the oven and transfer the
lamb to a serving platter. Cover loosely
with foil and rest for 30–40 minutes.
Strain the liquid from the pan into a
clear jug. The fat will rise to the top.
Skim most of it off with a spoon.
There should be 2–3 cups of sauce left.
Adjust salt, pepper, and lemon to taste.
Mix yogurt and preserved lemon or
lemon zest in a small bowl.

TO SERVE

Shred lamb with two forks.
Spread a bed of lemon yogurt on a
platter and top with the shredded lamb.
Spoon the roasting liquid over top.
Garnish with mint leaves.

Serve this delectable lamb with the Greenk Salad (page 72).

SALMON WITH SWEET CURRY RUB
and Lemongrass Coconut Sauce

This salmon has a salty-sweet spice rub and a creamy coconut curry sauce that you're going to love!
Serve it with some steamy basmati rice to soak it all up. Thanks to Colin Greenlaw for sharing this recipe during
the pandemic. We all stayed home for months, and some really good recipes came out of it! • SERVES 4

INGREDIENTS

Salmon and Rub

1 tbsp brown sugar
1 tsp curry powder
½ tsp onion powder
½ tsp garlic powder
½ tsp salt
1–2 tbsp olive oil
1½ lbs skin-on salmon, cut into portions

Coconut Curry Sauce

1 tbsp olive oil
2 cloves garlic, minced
1 tbsp ginger, peeled and finely grated
1 tbsp lemongrass paste
1 tbsp brown sugar
1 tsp red curry paste (or use up to 1 tbsp,
   depending on how hot you like it!)
1 can coconut milk
2 tbsp fish sauce
1 lime, zest and juice of
3 cups fresh spinach, chopped, loosely packed
½ cup cilantro, basil, mint or other
   fresh herbs, for garnish

METHOD

Salmon and Rub

Preheat oven to 475°F.
Place the oven rack in the top third of the oven.
Line a baking sheet with parchment paper or foil.
Make the rub by mixing dry ingredients and oil into a paste.
Place salmon skin side down on the pan
and rub the paste liberally over top.
Roast salmon for 6–12 minutes depending on preferred doneness.

Coconut Curry Sauce

Heat oil in a medium saucepan over medium heat.
Add garlic, ginger and lemongrass and sauté for 5 minutes.
Add sugar and curry paste and sauté for 3 minutes.
Mix in coconut milk, fish sauce, and lime zest and juice.
Stir in spinach until wilted. Remove pan from the heat.

TO SERVE

Place the salmon on a bed of basmati rice and spoon the sauce over.
Garnish with fresh herbs.

This sauce and rice would also be amazing
with your favourite white fish, sautéed prawns or scallops.

SHEET PAN CHICKEN

with Caramelized Shallots, Lemons and Medjool Dates

This is one of those go-to recipes you'll make over and over again. It's sweet and tangy and a little spicy, all from just a few ingredients. It's definitely got a weeknight-friendly vibe! • SERVES 4–6

INGREDIENTS

6–8 bone in chicken thighs
sea salt and freshly ground pepper
4 tbsp olive oil
½ tsp crushed red pepper ﬂakes
1 lemon, cut into thick rounds
4 shallots, halved lengthwise
6–8 garlic cloves, skins on
½ cup Castelvetrano olives
4 sprigs fresh thyme
8–10 Medjool dates, pitted

METHOD

Preheat oven to 375°F.

Place chicken on a parchment-lined baking sheet and season all over with salt and pepper to taste.

Drizzle with olive oil and sprinkle with pepper flakes.

Arrange lemon, shallots, garlic, olives and thyme around chicken.

Roast for 1 hour, or until chicken is cooked and brown, and lemon and shallots are slightly caramelized.

Add dates 15 minutes before chicken is finished cooking.

Remove from the oven. Remove the skins from the garlic and serve!

The dates add a nice sweetness to this chicken dish. Some potato gnocchi and the California Cucumber Salad (page 82) would be perfect with this simple chicken dish.

SPICED CHICKPEAS
with Sweet Potato Mash and Chimichurri

Something about the combination of all the spices, the sweetness of the mash, and the acidic chimichurri makes this dish so perfectly balanced! Have it as a main if you're a hungry vegan or as the perfect accompaniment to roast chicken. • SERVES 4

INGREDIENTS

Sweet Potatoes
4 medium-large sweet potatoes
2 tbsp olive oil, plus more for drizzling
sea salt and freshly ground pepper

Chimichurri Sauce
1 large handful mixed fresh herbs, such
  as parsley, cilantro or mint, chopped
¼ cup extra-virgin olive oil
1 tbsp red wine vinegar
2 cloves garlic, minced
1 tsp crushed red pepper flakes
sea salt and freshly ground pepper

Spiced Chickpeas
½ cup extra-virgin olive oil
2 15-oz cans chickpeas, drained
1 medium red onion, finely diced
4 garlic cloves, smashed
1 tsp onion powder
1 tbsp smoked paprika
1 tsp cumin
1 tsp turmeric
2 tbsp red wine vinegar

METHOD

Sweet Potatoes
Preheat oven to 400°F.
Place sweet potatoes on a parchment-lined baking sheet.
Drizzle with oil, sprinkle with salt and pepper to taste, and rub into sweet potato skins.
Roast for 50–60 minutes, or until a knife easily pierces the sweet potatoes.
Remove the sweet potatoes from the oven and slice them lengthwise.
Scoop out the sweet potato flesh into a medium-sized mixing bowl.
Mash with the 2 tbsp olive oil and salt and pepper to taste.

Chimichurri Sauce
Mix herbs, oil, vinegar, garlic and pepper flakes in a small bowl, and combine well. Season with salt and pepper to taste.

Chickpeas
Heat oil in a large frying pan over medium-high heat.
Rub chickpeas dry with a clean kitchen towel. Add chickpeas to oil and sauté for about 6 minutes, or until they start to lightly crisp.
Add onion and garlic, and cook for 4–6 minutes, stirring frequently, making sure garlic doesn't burn.
Stir in onion powder, smoked paprika, cumin and turmeric, and season with salt and pepper to taste.
Cook for an additional 2–4 minutes, stirring frequently until the spices are very fragrant but not burning.
Remove from the heat and stir in vinegar. If the chickpeas aren't as acidic as you'd like, add more vinegar!

TO SERVE

Create a base of the sweet potato mash.
Top with chickpea and onion mixture.
Place small spoonfuls of the chimichurri on top.

Conner made this chickpea and sweet potato dish for us one night, served with the most incredible, deboned split chicken, both drizzled with the chimichurri. We honestly thought it was one of the most amazing dinners we'd ever eaten!

PORTOBELLO BURGER
in Paradise

Sarah's favourite thing to eat in the world is a veggie burger! This one uses a full portobello cap and a slice of halloumi to make it filling and delicious. We made these in Hawaii recently, hence the name! • SERVES 4

INGREDIENTS

4 large whole portobello mushrooms
4 tbsp olive oil, divided
½ tsp sea salt, divided, plus more
½ tsp freshly ground pepper, plus more
½ medium yellow onion, sliced
1 red bell pepper, julienned
½ tsp dried oregano
1 6-oz piece halloumi, saganaki
   or similar frying cheese
½ cup mayonnaise
2 garlic cloves, minced
4 burger buns, preferably brioche
1 cup microgreens, arugula,
   or your favourite greens

METHOD

Preheat oven to 375°F.

Trim mushroom stems. Dice and reserve (optional).

Toss mushroom caps with 2 tbsp olive oil, and salt and pepper to taste.

Place mushrooms stem side up on a parchment-lined baking sheet, and bake for 20 minutes.

Heat 1 tbsp oil in a medium frying pan over medium-high heat.

Sauté onion for 2 minutes, then add diced mushroom stems, if using, and bell pepper.

Season with ¼ tsp salt and pepper to taste, and sprinkle with oregano.

Reduce heat to medium and cook, stirring frequently, for 4–6 minutes, or until everything is soft. Set aside in a small bowl.

Wipe down the pan, then heat the remaining 1 tbsp oil over medium heat.

Slice halloumi ¼-inch thick (4 slices) and pat it dry with a paper towel.

Fry the slices for 2 minutes per side, or until lightly browned, and set aside.

Mix mayonnaise and garlic in a medium bowl to make an aioli, and season with the remaining ¼ tsp salt and ½ tsp pepper.

Spread garlic aioli on both halves of the buns, then top with halloumi, mushrooms, fried pepper mixture and greens.

You could add a few strips of crispy bacon if you're like the "vegetarians" who ordered the Whitewater veggie burgers with bacon when Shelley ran the kitchen at the Fresh Tracks Café!

SWORDFISH
with Piccata Pan Sauce

This simple preparation of our favourite fish is so good and you're going to love it! Shelley makes it often in her little apartment at the Pink Palace with her funny little stove and kitchen. That's how simple and easy it is to make. There's a fabulous fish market in Ambleside that brings in the freshest of fish every day. Find some swordfish at your local fish store and make this! • SERVES 4

INGREDIENTS

2 large swordfish steaks (about 2 lbs),
   cut in half
sea salt and freshly ground pepper
4 tbsp all-purpose flour
2 tbsp olive oil
3 tbsp unsalted butter, divided
2 shallots, sliced thinly into rings
4 anchovy fillets, whole
2 tbsp capers, drained
½ cup white wine
¼ cup Italian parsley, finely chopped,
   for garnish
1 lemon, cut into wedges

METHOD

Season swordfish fillets with salt and pepper to taste, then dredge in flour.

Heat oil and 1 tbsp butter in a large frying pan over medium-high heat until hot.

Add swordfish fillets and sear until golden, about 3 minutes per side.

Set aside cooked swordfish to rest. Drain excess fat from the pan and discard.

Add the shallots, anchovies, capers and the remaining 2 tbsp butter to the still-hot pan.

Cook for about 3 minutes, or until shallots are softened.

Deglaze pan with wine and cook for about 2–3 minutes, or until alcohol cooks off and wine reduces.

Pour sauce evenly over the swordfish fillets and sprinkle with parsley.

Serve hot with lemon wedges on the side.

Any firm fresh fish would be delicious with this recipe!

Mya's Chicken Feta
PHYLLO PIE

Our friend Mya Mitchell made this amazing phyllo pie last fall when she was super busy with two little kids and needed a dinner that could feed her family for a few nights. For a healthy Kootenay mom with a full-time nursing career, a good dinner is definitely an important part of the week. We get that! Thanks Mya. • SERVES 8

INGREDIENTS

4 boneless, skinless chicken breasts
2 tbsp olive oil, divided
sea salt and freshly ground pepper
4 cloves garlic, minced
1 tbsp dried oregano
1 cup feta, crumbled
½ cup ricotta
2 cups frozen chopped spinach, thawed and drained until dry
½ cup green onions, chopped
2 eggs, beaten
4 tbsp fresh dill, chopped
4 tbsp fresh mint, chopped
½ tsp freshly ground pepper
9 sheets frozen phyllo pastry, thawed in the fridge overnight
½ cup butter, melted
1 tomato, diced
1 cup red onion, diced
½ cup pitted, chopped kalamata olives

METHOD

Preheat oven to 400°F.

Drizzle chicken with 1 tbsp oil. Season with salt, pepper, garlic and oregano.

Sear chicken breasts in a large frying pan over medium-high heat with the remaining 1 tbsp oil for about 5 minutes per side, or until golden brown.

Lower heat to low and cook chicken about 10 minutes, or until cooked through. Set aside to cool, cut into ½-inch-thick slices.

Mix cheeses, spinach, green onions, eggs, dill, mint and pepper in a large bowl.

Remove phyllo sheets and place on parchment paper or a clean counter surface. Cover with a clean kitchen towel to prevent them from drying out.

Brush 6 phyllo sheets with melted butter on both sides as you need each one.

Place each buttered sheet into a 9-inch springform pan, making sure it completely covers and hangs over the edges of the pan.

Spread half the spinach and feta mixture over the phyllo in the bottom of the pan.

Arrange the chicken slices on top, and then spread with the rest of the spinach feta mixture.

Press down tightly on the layers with a spatula or your hands.

Arrange tomato around the outer rim of the pie, followed by a ring of red onion and then olives in the centre.

Fold phyllo sheets from the edges of the pan to the centre. Cover the top of the pie with the remaining 3 sheets of buttered phyllo and tuck along the pan's edge with your fingers to make a nice lid.

Cover the pie with tinfoil and bake for 1 hour.

Remove tinfoil and bake for another 20 minutes, or until the top is golden brown.

Let rest for at least 30 minutes at room temperature.

Remove the pie from the springform pan, slice, and serve.

Serve with tzatziki and a classic Greek salad.
This is a winner dinner to take to a potluck — just reheat a bit when you get there!

The
ORCHID LIME BOWL

Back when the kids were little, Shelley and her friends used to go to a restaurant in Nelson and order this yummy bowl that they all loved. Moms and little toddlers in tow, they would all devour these bowls of peanutty goodness. • SERVES 4–6

INGREDIENTS

Dressing

½ cup smooth peanut butter
1 large or 2 small limes,
    juice and zest of
2 tsp sesame oil
4 tbsp sweet chili sauce
4 tbsp rice wine vinegar
4 tbsp tamari or soy sauce
1 tbsp maple syrup
4 cloves garlic, minced
2 tbsp ginger, peeled and grated
½ cup neutral oil, such as canola
    or avocado
½ cup chopped cilantro, divided

The Bowls

12–16 prawns, peeled
2 tbsp sea salt
6 peppercorns
1 bay leaf
1 16-oz package pad thai rice noodles
2 tbsp sesame oil
2 carrots, julienned
½ long English cucumber,
    de-seeded and julienned
1 red pepper, julienned
1 cup pea shoots
½ cup watermelon radishes,
    thinly sliced
½ cup fresh mint, chopped
½ cup cilantro, chopped
2 limes, quartered, for serving

Toasted Nuts

2 tbsp butter
1 cup slivered almonds
4 tbsp sesame seeds, toasted
½ tsp Chinese Šve spice
1 tsp salt
1 tsp sugar

METHOD

Dressing

Blend all dressing ingredients except oil and cilantro with an immersion blender or in a food processor until just combined.
Pour in a steady stream of oil while blending until incorporated.
Stir in half the cilantro and set aside.

Toasted Nuts

Melt butter in a heavy-bottomed pan over medium-high heat.
Add almonds, sesame seeds, Chinese five spice and salt and toss until golden brown.
Sprinkle sugar over and toss for another 30 seconds. Remove from heat and let cool.

The Bowls

Heat a pot of water to a boil and add salt, peppercorns and bay leaf.
Boil prawns for about 3 minutes, or until opaque. Remove from the boiling water and submerge in a bowl of ice water. When cooled, strain and set prawns aside.
Put noodles in a large bowl and cover with boiling water for 10 minutes, or until just tender.
Strain through a colander and rinse with cold water.
Return to the bowl and toss with sesame oil.

TO SERVE

Place noodles in individual serving bowls and pile with the vegetables and prawns.
Sprinkle with the nuts, mint and cilantro, then drizzle with the dressing.
Serve with quartered fresh limes to be squeezed over just before eating.

If poaching the prawns sounds like too much work, you can just buy pre-cooked prawns!

CHICKEN ENCHILADAS

with Queso Fresco and Toasted Pumpkin Seeds

Everyone needs a good chicken enchilada recipe. It's a great any-day-of-the-week comfort food dinner!
You can also substitute turkey for chicken if you need a way to use the leftover turkey at Christmas or Thanksgiving.
Both are amazing.   •   SERVES 6

INGREDIENTS

8 tbsp neutral oil, such as canola
  or avocado, divided
1 large onion, thinly sliced
4 cloves garlic, minced
2 jalapeno peppers, finely diced
  (about ¼ cup)
1 tsp ground cumin
1 28-oz can enchilada sauce, red or green
12 small yellow corn tortillas
3–4 cups shredded cooked chicken (store-
  bought rotisserie chicken is perfect!)
1 14-oz can pinto or black beans,
  drained and rinsed
3 cups Monterey Jack, grated, divided
¾ cup sour cream, plus more for serving
1 tsp sea salt
½ cup cilantro, chopped, for garnish
¾ cup queso fresco or cotija,
  crumbled, for garnish
½ cup pumpkin seeds, toasted,
  for garnish

METHOD

Preheat oven to 375°F.

Heat 2 tbsp of the oil in a large frying pan over medium-high heat.

Add onion, garlic and jalapeno, and cook for about 5 minutes, or until onion is soft, stirring frequently.

Stir in cumin and cook for another minute.

Pour in enchilada sauce and cook for about 8 minutes, or until slightly thickened.

Heat the remaining 6 tablespoons of oil in a medium-sized frying pan over medium-high heat until hot enough to lightly sizzle when you dip in a tortilla.

Dip each tortilla into oil, using tongs, making sure to cover it in oil, just until it's heated through, but not browned and still pliable.

Transfer to a plate lined with paper towels.

Mix chicken, beans and 2 cups of the Monterey Jack in a large mixing bowl.

Add 1 cup enchilada sauce mixture, sour cream and salt, and combine well.

Spread 1¼ cups enchilada sauce mixture across the bottom of a 9 × 13-inch baking pan.

Place a scoop of the chicken mixture in the centre of each tortilla, then roll up and place seam side down over the sauce. Repeat with the remaining tortillas.

Spread the remaining enchilada sauce mixture on top and sprinkle with the remaining 1 cup of Monterey Jack.

Bake for 25–30 minutes, or until cheese is bubbling and melted.

Garnish with cilantro, cheese and pumpkin seeds and serve with sour cream.

If you make these enchiladas with turkey instead of chicken,
throw in a little leftover stuffing if you have some. You'll be surprised how good this is!

Plate Lunch Miso Sake Glazed

BLACK COD

We died over this amazing glazed butterfish in a cute little plate lunch restaurant in the Diamond Head neighborhood of Honolulu last Christmas. We had to come home and recreate it so that we could eat it over and over again! Butterfish is oily and flaky like our sablefish or black cod here in BC, so we were thrilled that we could make something as delicious as that fish in Hawaii. We love to serve it with mashed potatoes and this wasabi drizzle, but plain basmati or sushi rice would be great too!   •   SERVES 4

INGREDIENTS

Fish and Marinade
4 6–8 oz black cod or
  sablefish fillets
¼ cup mirin
  (Japanese rice cooking wine)
¼ cup sake
½ cup sugar
½ cup white miso

Whipped Potatoes
10 medium Yukon Gold potatoes,
  peeled and quartered
1⅓ cup whole milk
6 garlic cloves, peeled and smashed
8 tbsp unsalted butter,
  room temperature
¼ cup sour cream
¼ cup fresh chives, finely chopped
1½ tsp sea salt, or to taste

Green Wasabi Drizzle
1 tsp wasabi paste
1 tbsp cilantro, chopped
1 tbsp fresh chives, chopped
1 tbsp yuzu juice or paste
¼ cup olive oil

METHOD

Fish and Marinade
Combine mirin, sake and sugar in a saucepan over medium heat, stirring to dissolve the sugar. Bring the mixture to a boil and turn heat down to low.
Add miso and simmer and whisk for 5–10 minutes, or until the marinade is smooth and caramel in colour. Remove from heat and cool completely.
Rinse fillets and pat really dry with a paper towel.
Place fillets in a glass dish or large sealable plastic bag and pour the cooled marinade over them.
Cover or seal the container and marinate in the fridge for at least an hour before cooking, or longer if you desire.
Preheat oven to 450°F and move rack to top third of oven.
Remove the fish from the marinade when ready to cook and shake off excess.
Place fish on a parchment-lined baking sheet.
Bake fish for 15–18 minutes, and then broil for 1–2 minutes until the top is deeply caramelized.

Whipped Potatoes
Put potatoes in a large pot and cover with cold water. Bring to a boil, then reduce heat to a simmer. Partially cover and cook for 15–18 minutes, or until potatoes are easily pierced with a fork.
Heat milk with garlic cloves until just steaming, then remove from heat and set aside. Remove garlic and discard.
Drain potatoes, keeping them in the pot. Keep the pot over very low heat and mash using a potato masher or electric mixer.
Drizzle in the warm milk when potatoes have reached your desired creaminess. Mix in butter, then stir in sour cream, chives and salt to taste.

Green Wasabi Drizzle
Mix all drizzle ingredients in a small bowl until combined.

TO SERVE
Spread a mound of the whipped potatoes on each serving plate.
Top with a piece of fish and drizzle with a spoonful of wasabi drizzle.

If you can find butterfish for this dish, lucky you! Salmon is also a winner with the marinade.

Salmoriglio
CHICKEN

Italians use salmoriglio on all sorts of grilled or roasted meats and veggies. It's lemony and has all the classic flavours you expect in an Italian dressing. You can assemble the entire recipe in the morning and just fling it into the oven before dinner. It's great served with a crunchy sourdough baguette to sop up all the juices! • SERVES 4–6

INGREDIENTS

Salmoriglio Dressing
2 lemons, zest and juice of
½ tsp crushed red pepper flakes
1 tsp dried oregano
4 garlic cloves, minced
¼ cup Italian parsley, finely chopped
¾ cup extra-virgin olive oil
¼ cup avocado oil or other neutral oil
sea salt and freshly ground pepper

Chicken
1 2½–3 lb whole chicken
1 red onion, diced
2 pepperoncini peppers, diced
1 cup green olives, preferably
   Cerignola or Castelvetrano,
   pitted and roughly chopped
1 28 oz can whole tomatoes
1 bunch lacinato kale, de-stemmed
   and torn into bite-sized pieces
3 tbsp white wine vinegar

METHOD

Salmoriglio Dressing
Mix lemon zest and juice, pepper flakes, oregano, garlic, and parsley in a large bowl.
Whisk in oils.
Season generously with salt and pepper to taste, and transfer half the dressing to a small bowl.

Chicken
Preheat the oven to 400°F.
Spatchcock chicken:
Set chicken on its breast so the back is facing you. Using a sharp knife or sturdy kitchen scissors, cut along one side of the backbone. Then cut along the other side of the backbone to remove it completely and discard. Turn chicken over. Press firmly with the heels of your hands or flat side of the knife to crack the breast bone so the chicken lies more or less flat.

Rub the salmoriglio from the small bowl all over the spatchcocked chicken.
Add onion, pepperoncini, olives, tomatoes (crushing them by hand) and their juices, kale and vinegar to the large bowl with the remaining salmoriglio.
Season with salt and pepper to taste.
Spread the vegetable mixture evenly on a parchment-lined baking sheet.
Place the spatchcocked chicken skin side up on the vegetables.
Roast in the oven for 50–60 minutes, or until chicken is cooked. Test by piercing the legs with a skewer; if the juices run clear, it's done.
Rest chicken for 10 minutes, then carve into legs, breasts and wings.
Serve chicken on the vegetables and sauce it cooked on.

Knowing how to spatchcock a chicken is a technique that comes in handy for many recipes, and it also impresses your friends and family!

SPICY PORK and FENNEL
Ragu

This is a classic Sunday night dinner for us. Let it cook all afternoon so you get to savour the aromas coming from your oven and end up with this delicious pasta meal. • SERVES 4–6

INGREDIENTS

1 2–2½ lb pork butt
2 tsp sea salt, plus more
freshly ground pepper
¼ cup olive oil
½ cup garlic cloves (about 20),
   peeled but left whole
2 tbsp fennel seeds, crushed to a powder
2 tsp crushed red pepper flakes
1 tbsp finely chopped jarred
   Calabrian peppers (or pepperoncini
   or cherry peppers)
1 cup white wine
2 28-oz cans whole tomatoes
20 basil leaves, coarsely chopped, divided
1 13-oz package tagliatelle pasta
3 oz Parmesan, finely grated

METHOD

Preheat oven to 350°F.
Season pork butt all over with
2 tsp salt and pepper.
Heat oil in a Dutch oven over
medium-high heat.
Sear pork for 10–12 minutes,
or until lightly browned on all sides.
Remove from the pot and set aside.
Add garlic, fennel, pepper flakes and
peppers to the Dutch oven and sauté
for 2 minutes, stirring to keep garlic
from burning.
Pour in wine to deglaze the pot
and cook for about 5 minutes to
reduce the alcohol.

Add canned tomatoes (crushing
them by hand) and their juices
to the pot.
Stir in half the basil, season with
salt and pepper to taste, and bring
back to a boil.
Return pork to the pot, cover, and
roast in the oven for 2½ hours.
Prepare pasta to package
instructions.
Remove pork from the oven and
shred while still in the pot, using
two forks.

TO SERVE

Ladle some of the pork and tomato sauce over tagliatelle in its pot
until noodles are well coated.
Plate the pasta and add another ladleful of the pork
and tomatoes over it.
Garnish with the remaining basil and a healthy portion of Parmesan.

You can use any type of pasta, but we prefer tagliatelle for this beautiful rich sauce.

YAKINIKU BEEF BOWL
with Yummy Pickles

We love this dish! You will too! It's a fusion of Japanese and Korean flavours with crunchy kimchi and cucumbers. It reminds us of eating at one of the amazing izakayas that you can find all over Vancouver. • SERVES 4–6

INGREDIENTS

1 2–2½ lb tri-tip roast or flank steak,
  silver skin removed
4 cloves garlic, grated
  on a microplane or minced
1 1-inch piece ginger,
  grated on a microplane
1 cup soy sauce
½ cup mirin
½ cup brown sugar
1 tbsp toasted sesame oil
2 tbsp gochujang
2 cups shiitake mushrooms, sliced
8 Persian cucumbers, very thinly
  sliced on a mandoline or
  with a sharp knife
1 tbsp sea salt
¼ cup rice vinegar
1 tbsp granulated sugar
1 tsp soy sauce
3 tbsp sesame seeds, toasted, divided
¼ cup pickled ginger
½ cup kimchi
2 cups short-grain white rice,
  prepared to package instructions

METHOD

Pat tri-tip dry and place in a sealable container for marinating.

Mix garlic, ginger, 1 cup soy sauce, mirin, brown sugar, oil and gochujang in a small pot.

Bring to a gentle boil and cook for 7 minutes to melt sugar and bring sauce together.

Cool the sauce entirely. Pour about ½ cup into the marinating container and use it to coat the tri-tip well. Refrigerate the rest of the sauce.

Seal the tri-tip container and marinate in the fridge for at least one hour or overnight.

Preheat oven to 350°F.

Put mushrooms in an ovenproof baking dish, pour about ⅓ cup of the sauce over them, and marinate for about 15 minutes.

Place the tri-tip on a foil- or parchment-lined baking sheet and roast for 45–50 minutes.

Put the marinated mushrooms and the reserved sauce in the oven for the last 10–15 minutes of the meat's cooking time.

Toss cucumbers with salt and set aside for 10 minutes to draw some liquid out of them.

Rinse cucumbers very well and squeeze out as much liquid as you can by wrapping them in a paper towel or clean kitchen towel and squeezing vigorously.

Whisk vinegar, granulated sugar, soy sauce, and 1 tbsp sesame seeds in a small mixing bowl.

Add cucumbers and toss well to coat.

Remove meat from the oven and let rest for 10 minutes before slicing very thinly against the grain.

Remove mushrooms from the oven and set aside.

Add the remaining 2 tbsp sesame seeds to the sauce, then spoon generous amounts over the sliced meat.

TO SERVE

Portion out some of the rice and top with lots of the tri-tip.

Arrange mushrooms, pickled cucumbers, pickled ginger and kimchi in the bowls.

We usually set out a bowl of the remaining sauce so people can add more because it's so friggin' delicious!

DESSERTS

◆

◆

CHEESECAKE

A divine pairing of two classic desserts, this creamy cheesecake is baked in a phyllo crust, topped with the classic baklava topping of chopped nuts and honey, and drizzled with honey syrup. This cheesecake is a thing of beauty! • SERVES 6–8

INGREDIENTS

Phyllo Crust

10 sheets frozen phyllo
pastry, thawed in the fridge
½ cup butter, melted
¼ cup sugar
¼ cup walnuts,
finely chopped

Cheesecake Filling

1¾ cups (400 g)
regular cream cheese,
room temperature
½ cup sugar
2 eggs, room temperature
1 tsp vanilla
½ cup sour cream

Honey-Nut Topping

¼ cup sugar
¼ cup water
½ cup honey
½ cup walnuts,
finely chopped
½ cup pistachios, toasted,
finely chopped

METHOD

Phyllo Crust

Preheat oven to 400°F.

Place thawed phyllo sheets on a clean counter.

Cover phyllo with a clean, damp kitchen towel while working to prevent it from drying out.

Lay the first sheet of the stack on the counter.

Brush the sheet thoroughly with some of the melted butter on one side and place into an 8-inch springform pan, pressing gently to cover the bottom and sides of the pan. The sheet will hang over the edge of the pan.

Sprinkle about 1 tsp sugar and 1 tsp walnuts on the first layer in the pan.

Lay the next sheet on the counter and brush with some butter. Place it to cover the first layer in the pan and sprinkle with about 1 tsp sugar and 1 tsp walnuts.

Repeat this process until you have used all 10 sheets.

Trim the overhanging pastry, leaving the edge even with the top of the pan.

Par-bake for 15 minutes, or until the pastry is a light golden colour. Remove from the oven and cool. Push down pastry that may have puffed up during baking.

Cheesecake Filling

Preheat oven to 325°F.

Process cream cheese in a food processor until smooth. Add sugar and pulse to combine.

Add one egg at a time, processing each well.

Scrape the processor's sides and bottom.

Add vanilla and sour cream and pulse until creamy.

Pour the filling into the par-baked crust. Bake about 1 hour or until the centre jiggles slightly.

Cool on a wire rack and then refrigerate to cool completely before spreading on the topping.

Honey-Nut Topping

Combine sugar, water and honey in a small pot over medium-high heat.

Bring to a boil, whisking continuously until it foams up, remove from heat and cool for 8–10 minutes.

Drizzle half of the syrup into the gaps between the cheesecake and the phyllo crust.

Add nuts to the remaining syrup. Heat to a boil, stirring continuously for 2 minutes.

Cool mixture for 8–10 minutes.

Spread mixture to the cake's edges.

Cool, release from springform pan and serve.

You can make this cheesecake the day before — just add the honey-nut topping a few hours before serving.

Salted Caramel
COOKIES

Who doesn't love salted caramel? The recipe for these delicious cookies calls for making your own caramel — trust us, it's easy! Thanks to Marianne for these dreamy cookies. • MAKES 18 COOKIES

INGREDIENTS

Caramel

1½ tbsp golden syrup
¾ cup granulated sugar
1½ tbsp butter
⅓ cup whipping cream

Cookies

1½ cups all-purpose flour
¾ tsp baking powder
½ tsp baking soda
½ tsp salt
½ cup butter,
   room temperature
⅓ cup granulated sugar
1 cup brown sugar
1 tsp vanilla
1 egg, room temperature
1 tbsp Maldon salt flakes,
   for sprinkling

METHOD

Caramel

Line a baking sheet with parchment paper.
Place all ingredients in a small, heavy-bottomed pot over medium-high heat and bring to a boil, whisking continuously.
Whisk until the mixture is a rich, golden brown and reduced by about half. This takes about 10 minutes. If you have a candy thermometer, the temperature should reach 250–275°F.
Remove immediately from heat, pour caramel onto a parchment-lined baking sheet and spread evenly with a spatula.
Allow to cool thoroughly. Once hard and completely cool, break into bite-sized chunks.

Cookies

Preheat oven to 350°F and line 2 cookie sheets with parchment paper.
Combine flour, baking powder, baking soda and salt in a bowl and set aside.
Cream butter until light and fluffy in a large mixing bowl. Add both sugars and vanilla and beat until incorporated.

Add egg and continue to beat until fluffy.
Gradually add the dry mixture to the wet and beat until just incorporated.
Mix in the caramel pieces until just incorporated.
Scoop out all the dough onto a prepared cookie sheet using a 1-oz (about 1½ tbsp) cookie scoop dipped in cold water.
Refrigerate the tray of cookie dough for at least an hour.
Transfer half the dough mounds to the second cookie sheet, ensuring that all are evenly distributed on both trays.
Bake for approximately 6 minutes. Slightly flatten the cookie mounds and rotate the pans.
Continue to bake for 11–13 minutes, or until the cookies are brown on the edges but still soft in the middle.
Remove from the oven and immediately sprinkle a few flakes of Maldon salt on top.
Cool cookies on the tray for 5–10 minutes before transferring to a wire cooling rack.

We always wonder who came up with the idea of combining caramel and salt. It sure is a winner!!

Lavender
HONEY LOAF

This extraordinary loaf comes from Sheri, the queen of bees.
She has five hives at her house and uses their honey and lavender from her garden to make
the best possible version of this recipe. Lavender and honey are meant to be together! • SERVES 6–8

INGREDIENTS

½ cup salted butter, room temperature
⅔ cup granulated sugar
2 eggs, room temperature
1 lemon, zest of
3 tbsp almond flour
1 cup plus 1 tbsp all-purpose flour
1¼ tsp baking powder
½ tsp salt
3 tbsp dried lavender flowers,
  lightly chopped, divided
½ cup honey

METHOD

Preheat oven to 325°F.

Line an 8 × 4-inch loaf pan with parchment paper.

Cream butter and sugar in a large bowl until pale and fluffy.

Add one egg at a time, beating between additions.

Add lemon zest, almond flour, all-purpose flour,
baking powder and salt. Beat to a smooth batter.

Stir in 1 tbsp lavender.

Spoon the mixture into the prepared loaf pan, smooth the
top, and bake for 40 minutes, or until a toothpick
comes out clean.

Mix honey and the remaining 2 tbsp lavender in a small
pot over low heat. Steep for a few minutes and then strain
through a fine-mesh strainer.

Remove the loaf pan from the oven and set on a wire rack.
While the loaf is still warm, pierce the cake to three-quarters
of its depth with a skewer, creating holes all over the top.

Slowly pour the lavender honey over the surface, allowing
it to soak in.

Remove the loaf from the pan and cool right side up
on the rack.

You can use fresh lavender flowers or store-bought, depending on the time of year.

LEMON SHORTBREAD

Shortbread is the perfect buttery, tender and crumbly cookie that can be eaten year-round. There are so many shortbread recipes to choose from, and this one shared by the adorable Barb Gosney is our go-to! The shortbread can be eaten straight-up without the icing or decorate it with little sprinkles to make it more festive. • MAKES 16 COOKIES

INGREDIENTS

Lemon Shortbread

1 cup almond or gluten-free flour
1 cup rice flour
½ cup plus 2 tbsp icing sugar, sifted
½ tsp sea salt
1 cup butter, room temperature
1 tbsp lemon zest
1 tbsp freshly squeezed lemon juice

Lemon Icing

½ cup icing sugar, sifted
1 tbsp freshly squeezed lemon juice

METHOD

Lemon Shortbread

Preheat oven to 325°F.

Sift flours, icing sugar and salt into a mixing bowl.

Cream butter until light in a separate bowl.

Mix in the flour mixture until well incorporated.

Add lemon zest and juice and mix well.

Form dough into a ball. Wrap in plastic wrap and refrigerate for 30 minutes.

Line a 9-inch round fluted tart pan or a 9 × 9-inch baking pan with parchment paper.

Press dough evenly into the pan and prick all over with a fork.

Bake for 30–35 minutes.

Cool completely before drizzling with the lemon icing.

Cut into slices.

Lemon Icing

Mix icing sugar and lemon juice together in a small bowl until thick enough to coat the back of a spoon.

Drizzle on the shortbread.

144

It doesn't have to be Christmas to make these lemony shortbread treats!
They're gluten free, which is a bonus for those who avoid gluten.

Raspberry Cornmeal Buttermilk
MUFFINS

We love cornmeal and buttermilk together. These muffins are perfect when you need a little not-too-sweet snack
with a cup of tea or coffee. They're also a great breakfast option with a nice piece of cheddar or spread with ricotta cheese.
Swapping blackberries for the raspberries is also really lovely. • MAKES 9 LARGE or 12 SMALL MUFFINS

INGREDIENTS

1½ cups all-purpose flour
¾ cup cornmeal
¾ cup granulated sugar
2¼ tsp baking powder
½ tsp baking soda
¼ tsp salt
2 eggs, room temperature, lightly beaten
⅓ cup neutral oil, such as canola
1 cup buttermilk
1 tsp vanilla
1 lemon, zest of
2 cups fresh or frozen raspberries, divided

METHOD

Preheat oven to 400°F.

Grease muffin tin with butter or line with paper muffin cups.

Combine flour, cornmeal, sugar, baking powder, baking soda and salt in a large mixing bowl. Make a well in the centre of the mixture.

Mix eggs, oil, buttermilk, vanilla and lemon zest well in a separate bowl.

Gently mix the wet ingredients into the dry ingredients until just incorporated. Do not overmix.

Scoop 2 tbsp of the batter into the bottom of each muffin cup. Lightly press 4 raspberries into each muffin. Top with another 2 tbsp of batter, spreading slightly to seal in the raspberries underneath. Top with the remaining raspberries.

Bake on the middle rack of the oven for about 20–22 minutes, rotating the pan halfway through baking. The muffins are done when a skewer or toothpick comes out clean.

Set the muffin tin on a wire rack for 5 minutes before turning out the muffins to cool.

These scrumptious muffins come from Emmy, the queen of baking!

BANANA CAKE
with Chocolate Hazelnut Mascarpone Cream

This is a super-easy layer cake with no buttercream icing or smooth edges to fiddle with. We love banana cake, and the addition of the chocolate hazelnut spread and mascarpone reminds us a bit of tiramisu. Easiest cake ever! • SERVES 8

INGREDIENTS

Cake
2 eggs, room temperature
1 cup granulated sugar
2 tbsp brown sugar
½ cup neutral oil,
    such as canola
1⅓ cups mashed ripe bananas
    (about 3½ bananas)
2 tbsp full-fat plain
    Greek yogurt, or sour cream
1 tsp vanilla
1½ cups all-purpose flour
1 tsp baking soda
½ tsp cinnamon
¼ tsp salt

Chocolate Hazelnut Mascarpone Cream
1 cup mascarpone
1 cup whipping cream
2 tbsp granulated sugar
⅓ cup chocolate hazelnut
    spread (Nutella or your
    favourite brand)
cocoa powder, for dusting

METHOD

Cake
Preheat oven to 325°F.
Grease bottoms of two 8-inch round baking pans and line with parchment paper.
Beat eggs and both sugars together using an electric mixer on high speed for about 5 minutes, or until pale and thick.
Turn down the mixer to medium speed and slowly drizzle in oil until incorporated.
Fold in mashed bananas, yogurt and vanilla.
Sift flour, baking soda, cinnamon and salt together in a bowl, then fold gently into the banana mixture.

Divide the batter between the two prepared cake pans and bake for 30–35 minutes, or until the cakes are golden brown and a skewer inserted into the centre comes out clean.
Cool on a wire rack before inverting out of the pan onto a baking sheet.

Chocolate Hazelnut Mascarpone Cream
Whip mascarpone, whipping cream and sugar together using an electric mixer on high speed until thick and almost-stiff peaks form.
Divide the cream equally into two bowls.
Gently fold the chocolate hazelnut spread into one bowl of cream so there are still swirls through the cream. Leave the other bowl plain.

TO ASSEMBLE

Place one layer of cake on a serving platter.
Top with the plain cream and spread almost to the edges.
Place the other layer on top, pressing down slightly.
Top with the swirled chocolate hazelnut cream, spreading it out to the edges.
Dust lightly with cocoa powder.
Refrigerate until ready to serve.

This may sound weird, but try substituting the chocolate hazelnut spread with your favourite smooth peanut butter. Mike Adams loves the combo of peanut butter and bananas more than anyone!

KEY LIME PIE

When there's no fruit in season for a fresh fruit pie, key lime pie is always a great choice. This one is magical because of the coconut oil in the crust and because it's made with sweetened condensed milk, which gives it the creamiest texture. You could make 8 tarts if you'd rather have little individual ones. • SERVES 8

INGREDIENTS

Crust
1½ cups graham crumbs
4 tbsp coconut oil, melted
2 tbsp unsalted butter, melted
1 tbsp sugar
¾ tsp salt

Filling
4 large egg yolks, room temperature
1 10-oz can sweetened condensed milk
2 tsp lime zest, plus more for garnish
1 cup freshly squeezed lime juice
    (from 8–10 limes; key limes are best
    if you can find them)
pinch salt

Topping
1 cup whipping cream
¼ cup icing sugar
1 cup full-fat Greek yogurt or sour cream

METHOD

Crust
Preheat oven to 350°F.
Mix all the crust ingredients until you've got really moist crumbs.
Press the crumb mixture into a 9-inch pie plate and bake for 9–12 minutes, or until the crust starts to lightly brown around the edges.
Remove from the oven and set aside to cool. Leave the oven on.

Filling
Whisk egg yolks in a large bowl for about 3 minutes, or until pale and fluffy.
Add condensed milk and whisk a few more minutes until the mixture is light and airy.
Fold in lime zest and juice, and salt using a spatula or wooden spoon.
Pour mixture into the partially cooked pie crust and return to the oven for another 25–30 minutes, or until the centre just barely jiggles. The top shouldn't brown, so keep an eye on it!
Remove the pie from the oven and cool completely. Refrigerate it if you want to speed up the cooling.

Topping
Whip cream and icing sugar until medium peaks form.
Place yogurt in a large bowl.
Fold the whipped cream gently into the yogurt.
Spread over the cooled pie and sprinkle with more lime zest.

The crust can be made the day before. You can also make the filling ahead, but store it separately, not on the crust. All you have to do the next day is bake the pie, make the topping and assemble!

TEA BITES

We love having little treats on hand that require super-low effort. If you do too, then you'll love these no-bake bites!
They're the perfect little snack to have with a cup of tea. • MAKES 12 LITTLE COOKIES

INGREDIENTS

1 cup organic shredded coconut
1 cup organic almond flour
¼ tsp table salt
⅓ cup coconut oil, melted
⅓ cup agave nectar
½ tsp vanilla
⅓ cup chocolate chips

METHOD

Mix coconut, almond flour
and salt in a small bowl.
Combine wet ingredients in
a medium-sized bowl.
Add the dry ingredients and mix well.
Stir in chocolate chips.
Press into mini muffin tins.
Freeze for one hour.

The coconut is also really good toasted!
Keep the bites in a sealable container or plastic bag in the freezer.

Epiphany Cakes'
VEGAN CARROT CAKE

This is the absolutely amazing vegan carrot cake from Epiphany Cakes in Nelson.
It was Conner and Sarah's wedding cake last July on the beach. The decorating was like nothing you've ever seen before!
Thanks so much Melissa Owen for sharing your recipe, which we have reproduced here. • SERVES 6–8

INGREDIENTS

Vegan Carrot Cake

½ cup vegetable oil
1 cup sugar
2 teaspoons vanilla
1 cup coconut milk,
    well mixed
½ cup unsweetened
    apple sauce
2 cups organic carrots,
    grated
2¼ cups all-purpose flour
1 tsp salt
3 tsp baking powder
1 tsp baking soda
2 tsp cinnamon
1 tsp powdered ginger
½ tsp nutmeg

Aquafaba Vanilla Icing

1 540 ml can of
    organic chickpeas
1¼ cups granulated sugar
2 cups vegan butter,
    room temperature
2 tsp vanilla extract

METHOD

Cake

Preheat oven to 350°F.

Prepare an 8 x 8-inch pan by spraying thoroughly with pan spray and lining with parchment paper.

Put the oil, sugar, vanilla, coconut milk and applesauce in a large bowl and whisk to combine.

Fold in the grated carrots.

Sift together the flour, salt, baking powder, baking soda and spices into a bowl.

Add the dry ingredients into the bowl with the carrot mixture and fold gently until combined and no streaks of flour are visible.

Transfer batter to the prepared baking pan.

Bake for 40–45 minutes, until a knife inserted in the centre of the cake comes out clean.

Remove from the oven and allow to cool completely on a cooling rack before decorating with Aquafaba Vanilla Icing.

Aquafaba Vanilla Icing

Strain the chickpeas and reserve the liquid from the can. You should end up with about 1 cup of aquafaba.

Combine the aquafaba and the sugar in the bowl of your stand mixer.

Place the mixing bowl on a pot of simmering water and whisk by hand for 8–10 minutes, until the sugar granules are dissolved (test it by rubbing the mixture between your fingers).

Beat the aquafaba mixture using the whisk attachment on medium speed until you have stiff peaks — this will take a while! Once the mixture has thickened a bit you can turn the mixer up to high to expedite the process (if you put it on high too soon, the chickpea liquid will splash all over the place and make a mess).

Add the vegan butter one tablespoon at a time once you've got stiff peaks and continue mixing on high speed. At this point the icing will likely split, curdle, and look like a disastrous mess. Don't worry, just keep mixing on high speed. The icing will eventually come together.

Add the vanilla and use immediately.

Note: Stiff peaks are when, after much whisking, your meringue becomes thick and glossy, holds its shape, and points straight up without collapsing when the whisk is turned upside down.

"Aquafaba" is the name for the liquid in a can of chickpeas. I'm not sure who discovered that it could be used to create a vegan meringue, but whoever it was deserves a prize for ingenuity. This icing is by far the best non-dairy icing I've ever tried. It's smooth, creamy and easy to work with. The preparation requires a stand mixer and a bit of patience, but it's well worth it. And it's also dairy free and vegan!

A Tip from Whitewater Cooks: Make your favourite cream cheese icing for this cake if you'd rather!

Irish Coffee
CUPCAKES

Who doesn't love a bit of Baileys in their coffee!? Our friend Patti Mitchell is a really good baker and the queen of cupcakes, and she shared this recipe with us. These unforgettable cupcakes are the perfect pairing with an after-dinner espresso.

• MAKES 12 CUPCAKES •

INGREDIENTS

Cupcakes
1½ cups all-purpose flour
1 cup granulated sugar
¼ cup plus 2 tbsp
  unsweetened cocoa powder
¾ tsp baking soda
½ tsp baking powder
½ tsp salt
½ cup neutral oil such as canola
¼ cup strong brewed coffee
  or espresso, cooled
¼ cup Baileys Original Irish Cream
  liqueur
2 eggs, room temperature, beaten
½ cup sour cream
½ tsp vanilla
chocolate-covered espresso beans,
  for garnish

Kahlúa Cream Filling
½ cup whipping cream
2 tbsp granulated sugar
1½ tbsp cream cheese, room temperature
1 tbsp Kahlúa Coffee Liqueur

Baileys Buttercream Icing
¼ cup butter, softened
¼ cup cream cheese, room temperature
2¾ cups icing sugar, sifted
¼ cup Baileys

METHOD

Cupcakes
Preheat oven to 350°F.
Line muffin tin cups with liners.
Whisk flour, sugar, cocoa powder, baking soda, baking powder, and salt together in a large bowl.
Mix oil, coffee, Baileys and eggs in a separate bowl.
Add to dry ingredients and beat with an electric mixer on medium speed until smooth.
Mix in sour cream and vanilla.
Spoon the batter evenly into the muffin tins, filling each two-thirds full.
Bake for about 16–18 minutes, or until a skewer comes out clean.
Cool in the muffin tin on a wire rack for 5 minutes, then remove cupcakes and cool completely on wire racks.

Kahlúa Cream Filling
Whip cream until very stiff, adding in sugar gradually once the cream reaches the soft peaks stage.
Beat cream cheese on medium speed until smooth in a medium-sized bowl.
Mix in Kahlúa slowly, then fold in the whipped cream.
Chill covered until needed.

Baileys Buttercream Icing
Beat butter and cream cheese with an electric mixer on medium speed until creamy.
Reduce the mixer speed and gradually add icing sugar, beating until smooth, and then mix in Baileys.

TO ASSEMBLE
Spoon the cream filling into a pastry bag. Fit it with a long narrow tip, then insert it into the top of each cupcake and squeeze about 1 tbsp of filling into the centre. You can also poke a hole in each cupcake with your finger and place a teaspoon of filling in each hole.
Pipe or spread the buttercream icing on top of the cupcakes and garnish with chocolate covered espresso beans.

A sprinkle of Maldon sea salt flakes instead of the espresso beans is also really yummy!

BLOOD ORANGE and CARDAMOM CAKE

This feisty orange cake is so orangey and moist, you'll want to eat it for breakfast!
Gail Morrison, literally the queen of cheeriness, shared this recipe with us on a ski trip this year and
we couldn't wait to try it. It's definitely a spunky one, just like our amazing friend Gaily. • SERVES 12

INGREDIENTS

1 cup unsalted butter, room temperature,
  plus more for greasing the pan
1¼ cups granulated sugar
3 large eggs, room temperature
2 blood oranges or regular oranges
  (about 1 lb), peeled, ends trimmed,
  cut into chunks and de-seeded
2 tbsp plus 1 tsp freshly squeezed orange juice
  (about ½ orange)
2½ cups all-purpose flour
¼ tsp salt
¼ tsp baking soda
½ tsp baking powder
½ tsp ground cardamom
1½ cups icing sugar

METHOD

Preheat oven to 325°F.
Butter a 9-inch springform pan.
Cream butter and sugar in a large bowl with
an electric mixer until light.
Mix in eggs one at a time until combined.
Pulse orange chunks in a food processor until mostly
smooth but not puréed.
Mix 1½ cups of the processed orange until blended
into the batter. (Set aside the remainder for another use.)
Combine flour, salt, baking soda, baking powder and
cardamom and beat into batter until just smooth.
Scrape the batter into the prepared baking sheet and
smooth the top.
Bake for about 55 minutes, or until the cake is risen
and firm to the touch, and a toothpick comes out clean
with just a few crumbs clinging.
Cool the pan on a rack set over a baking sheet for
ten minutes, then invert the cake onto the rack and
cool completely.
Whisk icing sugar and orange juice in a small bowl.
Spoon the glaze over the cake once it's cooled. Let the
glaze set, then slice and serve.

For a more festive version of this cake, ice it with our favourite cream cheese icing! To make the optional icing,
cream together ½ cup room temperature cream cheese and ¼ cup room temperature butter until smooth.
Mix in 1 tsp vanilla. Beat in 3 cups of icing sugar, ½ cup at a time, until well combined.

Lisa Shippy is such a great cook and entertainer, and a finder of easy and tasty recipes! She shared this caramel sauce and sundae idea with Shelley while riding up the chairlift this winter. Our other fave sauce for topping sundaes is Nanny Vance's chocolate sauce. Top with both sauces — or one or the other — and you're golden! Sprinkle with our Chinese Five-Spice Toasted Nuts and toasted coconut ribbons, and you've got a sundae! Be sure to have your favourite vanilla ice cream in the freezer at all times.

• EACH SAUCE MAKES ABOUT 1 CUP •

INGREDIENTS

Lisa's Date Caramel Sauce

Makes about 1 cup
8 Medjool dates, pitted
½ cup full-fat coconut milk
⅓ cup maple syrup

Nanny Vance's
Easy Chocolate Sauce

1 cup granulated sugar
½ cup cocoa powder
⅛ tsp salt
½ cup boiling water
¼ cup butter, cut into chunks
1 tsp vanilla

Chinese Five-Spice
Toasted Nuts

2 tbsp butter
1 cup slivered almonds
4 tbsp sesame seeds, toasted
½ tsp Chinese Šve spice
1 tsp salt
1 tsp sugar

METHOD

Lisa's Date Caramel Sauce

Process all ingredients in a food processor until smooth and creamy.

Add a bit more coconut milk if the sauce is too thick.

Store in a Mason jar or sealable plastic container in the fridge.

Nanny Vance's
Easy Chocolate Sauce

Place sugar, cocoa powder and salt in a small sauce pot.

Add boiling water and butter chunks.

Bring to a rolling boil for one minute, stirring constantly.

Remove from heat and stir in vanilla.

Chinese Five-Spice Toasted Nuts

Melt butter in a heavy-bottomed pan, then add almonds, sesame seeds, Chinese five spice and salt.

Toss for about 3–4 minutes, or until golden brown.

Add sugar and toss for another 30 seconds.

Remove from heat and allow to cool thoroughly.

Store in a jar or plastic bag.

This may seem like the easiest dessert recipe in the world, and it is — that's why we like it! To make it even more delicious you could add toasted coconut ribbons. Pick your favourite vanilla ice cream and you've got your every-day-of-the-week sundae! Double or triple this recipe if you want a bigger batch. The sauces keep in the fridge for two weeks or more.

Gail"s

HERO COOKIES

Gail is famous for her cookies! Her lucky husband, Paul, always has a supply of her treasured cookies in the cookie jar. These are his favourites, and Paul is Gail's hero. • MAKES ABOUT 24 COOKIES

INGREDIENTS

1½ cups unbleached all-purpose flour
1 tsp baking powder
½ tsp baking soda
1 tsp salt
14 tbsp (7 oz) unsalted butter,
    room temperature
¾ cup granulated sugar
½ cup light brown sugar
1 egg, room temperature
1 tsp vanilla
1 cup granola
1 cup chocolate chips
½ cup crushed salted pretzel pieces
½ cup chopped pecans

METHOD

Preheat oven to 350°F.

Line cookie sheet(s) with parchment paper.

Sift flour, baking powder, baking soda and salt into a medium-sized bowl and set aside.

Beat butter and sugars in a large bowl with an electric mixer at medium-low speed until just combined.

Scrape the bowl with a rubber spatula. Add egg and vanilla and beat again. Scrape bowl again.

Mix in flour mixture until just incorporated and smooth.

Stir in granola, chocolate chips, pretzels and nuts until evenly distributed.

Refrigerate the dough at least 1 hour before baking.

Scoop dough into balls using a 1-oz cookie scoop (about 1½ tbsp each). Place on the prepared baking sheet about 2½ inches apart (10–11 cookies per baking sheet).

Bake one sheet at a time for 15–18 minutes, or until cookies are a deep golden brown, rotating the pan halfway through baking.

Cool completely on the pan before moving the cookies to a wire rack.

We love these sweet and salty cookies — they'll definitely become one of your go-to favourites!

INDEX

WHITEWATER COOKS
the food we love